What Will I Do With

All Those Green Vegetables?

Elaine Borish, an American living in London, was born in New York City. She holds degrees from Rutgers, Boston University, and Northeastern University and has taught at universities in New England. In Old England, she has lectured in English and American literature at Morley College in London. Her numerous articles have appeared in leading newspapers and magazines.

Also by Elaine Borish

A Legacy of Names
Literary Lodgings
Novel Cuisine
This Book Is Unpublishable!
What Will I Do With All Those Courgettes?
What Will I Do With All Those Root Vegetables?

Elaine Borish

What Will I Do With All Those Green Vegetables?

Fidelio Press

Telluride · London

Dedicated to all cultivators and consumers of green vegetables—and to my favorite man with a hoe.

Published by
Fidelio Press, Inc.
120 Aldasoro Road
Telluride CO 81435

Printed in U.K.

Cover Design by Kate Chitham

PREFACE

Vegetables are an ongoing feature of our culinary world, with most varieties available to us most of the year round. But the home grower can obtain the youngest and freshest crop and thereby enjoy the full flavor of these real delicacies.

After publication of my first volume, *What Will I Do With All Those Courgettes?* friends and gardening acquaintances began to entreat: But what should I do with my parsnips? Or Jerusalem artichokes? I grew too many carrots. . . a bumper crop of beets . . . My family is tired of all those. . . And so on. The litany left me with little choice but to write a second volume of easy-to-prepare recipes for easy-to-grow vegetables—*What Will I Do With All Those Root Vegetables?*

But green vegetables also arrive in profusion and also need a suitable culinary outlet. Hence, my third volume—*What Will I Do With All Those Green Vegetables?* It aims to make successful and satisfying use of all those beans and broccoli, sprouts and spinach. It omits products that thrive in tropical climates (such as okra), and it avoids highly complicated concoctions (such as veggies in brioche).

I have tried to offer recipes that are less ordinary and that will go a long way toward using up your crop while producing festive food for your table.

In specifying recipe quantities or instructions, my favorite word remains "about" because preparation should be easy and fun. I still believe that undue concern for exactness should not outweigh your own logical application.

Contents

Artichokes

ARTICHOKES

Artichokes, or globe artichokes as they are also known, are a very delicious and sociable food to eat. Using the fingers eliminates any notion of formality. One dips the leaf into sauce, then draws it through the front teeth, eating the fleshy part and discarding the rest of the leaf and the prickly choke on the plate. At the centre of this delectable vegetable is the heart, eaten with a knife and fork.

These members of the thistle family, with their spiky leaves and fuzzy choke, intimidate many people, but those who manage to get to the sweet and tender heart are richly rewarded with a delicacy for a prize. They also receive the benefits of magnesium, potassium, and fiber.

Artichoke hearts, or bottoms, are the innermost part of the vegetable, without the outer leaves or choke. It is fun to eat the meat on the leaves (which is just as delicious as the heart), but the interior heart is what the vegetable is all about. That is why most recipes trim off the outer parts and deal with just the heart.

Artichokes have been growing around the Mediterranean for centuries. Said to have originated in Italy, they are nowadays grown all over southern Europe and in California. But they are worth cultivating in more temperate climates as they are best when eaten as soon as possible after harvesting. Make no mistake, you can use tinned or jarred artichoke hearts, but the flavor will not be the same as good, fresh artichokes.

RECIPES for ARTICHOKES

Steamed Artichokes

*It is best to steam artichokes as they may become
waterlogged if boiled in water.*

**4 large or 12 very small artichokes
a few sprigs of fresh tarragon or thyme (optional)
salt and pepper**

1. Using a scissors or large knife, trim off the tops to about a half inch (1.2 cm) from the artichokes. Using a paring knife, peel around the base and cut off the bottom ¼ inch (.6 cm). Break off any rough exterior leaves.
2. Place in a steamer bottom up and add herbs if you want to. Cover and cook 20 to 40 minutes. The artichokes are done when an outer leaf pulls off easily and the flesh on it is tender.
3. Drain them upside down for a minute or two before serving hot. Or store upside down for later serving. Serve hot with melted butter, or at room temperature with vinaigrette. If serving cold, you may use mayonnaise or French dressing. Lemon juice may accompany artichokes at any temperature.

Serves 4

Artichokes A La Grecque

This salad makes a lovely starter.

4 medium artichokes
24 fl oz (700 ml or 3 cups) water
juice of one lemon
4 fl oz (100 ml or ½ cup) olive oil
salt to taste
1 stalk celery, minced
1 branch fennel, minced (optional)
few coriander seeds
4 or 5 peppercorns

1. Cut the artichokes into quarters. Remove the prickly choke and trim off the pointed ends of the leaves until they are about 1 inch (2.5 cm) long.
2. Mix the remaining ingredients and bring to a boil. Add the artichokes. Cover and cook until tender, about 15-20 minutes.
3. Cool the artichokes in the cooking liquid and serve in it.

Serves 4

Sautéed Artichoke Hearts

The choke need not be removed from very small artichokes, but large artichokes will take a bit longer to prepare. You can transform this recipe into a dish of curried artichoke hearts by simply adding a teaspoon (or less) of curry powder to the oil.

4 large or 12 very small artichokes
4 tablespoons olive oil
1 clove garlic, mashed (optional)
flour for dredging
salt and pepper to taste
minced fresh parsley leaves for garnish
lemon wedges

1. If using large artichokes, cut them into halves or quarters, remove leaves and chokes, and trim the bottoms. With small artichokes, just peel off all the leaves and trim the bottoms.
2. Place them in boiling water to cover. Lower heat and simmer until just tender, from 6 to 20 minutes depending on size. When done, plunge them into ice water. Drain and dry the hearts. The recipe may be prepared in advance up to this point, then refrigerated in a covered container for up to two days before continuing.
3. Place the oil in a large frying pan on medium-high heat. Add the garlic if you want to.

4. Dredge each heart in flour and shake off the excess. Place in frying pan and cook, turning once or twice until nicely browned all over, about 10 minutes. Season with salt and pepper.
5. Serve hot, garnished with parsley and accompanied by lemon wedges.

Serves 4

Braised Artichokes with Tarragon

This recipe requires no pre-cooking. Simply clean the artichokes, cook them for a few minutes in oil, and finish them with liquid.

4 large or 12 very small artichokes
3 tablespoons olive oil
1 tablespoon minced garlic
1 tablespoon minced fresh tarragon leaves or 1 teaspoon dried
8 fl oz (225 ml or 1 cup) chicken or vegetable stock or water
salt and pepper to taste
1 tablespoon lemon juice
chopped fresh parsley leaves for garnish

1. Cut large artichokes into halves or quarters, remove the leaves and chokes, and trim the bottoms. If you are using very small artichokes, just peel off the leaves and trim the bottoms, ignoring the chokes.
2. Heat oil in a large frying pan together with the garlic until the garlic begins to color, about 5 minutes. Add the artichokes and cook for about 5 minutes, stirring occasionally. Add the tarragon and stock or water. Bring to a boil, cover, and turn heat to medium-low. Cook for about 10 minutes, then turn the artichokes.
3. Cook for about 15-30 minutes, checking for tenderness about every 5 minutes.

4. When the artichokes are tender, add the salt and freshly ground black pepper. If there is too much liquid, raise the heat to high for a few minutes to reduce the liquid.
5. Before serving, sprinkle with lemon juice and parsley.

Serves 4

Easy Artichokes

These artichokes, with a touch of color, are equally good eaten hot or cold.

6 artichokes
3 carrots, peeled and finely diced
1 medium onion, peeled and finely diced
4 fl oz (100 ml or ½ cup) olive oil
3-4 tablespoons chopped fresh parsley
2 fl oz (50 ml or ¼ cup) lemon juice
1 tablespoon dried oregano
1 tablespoon dried basil
1 teaspoon freshly ground black pepper
salt to taste

1. Place artichokes in a large pot and fill with water to just cover. Add remaining ingredients. With pot partially covered, cook at a gentle boil for about 40 minutes or until leaves pull away easily.
2. Remove artichokes to a large serving dish. Strain cooking liquid and sprinkle vegetables and herbs over artichokes. Serve hot. Or allow to cool and serve at room temperature.

Serves 6

Roasted Artichokes

Don't let artichokes intimidate you, as they provide pleasurable eating experiences such as this delicious side dish.

4 artichokes
lemon juice
4 fl oz (100 ml or ½ cup) dry white wine
2 teaspoons thyme, crushed
1 teaspoon olive oil
salt and pepper to taste
2 bay leaves

1. Trim the artichokes by cutting about 1 inch (1.25 cm) off the tops. Cut the stems off the base. Cut the artichokes into sixths and place them in a large bowl of cold water with lemon juice.
2. In a bowl, mix together the white wine, thyme, olive oil and salt and pepper.
3. Remove artichokes from bowl of water and lemon juice. Pat dry with paper towels. Place them in the white wine mixture and toss them around until they are well coated.
4. Arrange artichokes in a single layer in a greased baking dish. Sprinkle any remaining wine mixture over them. Place bay leaves, broken into halves, between the artichokes. Cover with aluminum foil.
5. Bake for 30 minutes in a hot oven at 400°F (200°C). Remove foil covering. Bake for another 20 minutes or until edges are crisp and beginning to brown. Discard bay leaves. Serve with French or ranch dressing.

Serves 4

Beef-Stuffed Artichokes

This elegant vegetable can be used to make a main course that is a rare treat.

6 artichokes
1 tablespoon butter
¾ lb (325 g) ground beef
1 small-medium onion, chopped
3 tablespoons fresh parsley, chopped
3 oz (75 g) bread crumbs
1 egg
1 teaspoon salt
freshly ground black pepper to taste
¼ teaspoon powdered ginger
¼ teaspoon crumbled oregano leaves
6 slices fresh tomato
2 tablespoons olive oil
2 tablespoons buttered bread crumbs
2 tablespoons lemon juice.

1. Prepare artichokes for stuffing: Wash and cut off the top third with a sharp knife or scissors. Pull off the tough outside leaves and discard. Open the center leaves carefully with the fingers. Then turn the artichoke over on a flat surface and press down firmly to make the leaves spread open further. Turn the artichoke right side up and pull the yellowish leaves from the center. Sprinkle with lemon juice to retain the color. Use a soup spoon to carefully scrape and pull out all of the prickly

part, or choke, from the heart. Sprinkle additional juice over the scraped artichoke bottom. Finally, cut the stem off the base with a sharp knife.

2. Heat the butter in a frying pan, add the beef and onion and sauté until browned. Remove from heat. Mix in the parsley, bread crumbs, beaten egg, salt, pepper, ginger and oregano. Spoon this filling into the artichoke centers and add a slice of tomato on top.

3. Brush olive oil over the artichokes and tomatoes. Place them in a baking pan so that they fit snugly together and sprinkle with buttered crumbs.

4. Fill the pan with boiling water to the depth of one inch (2.5 cm) and add lemon juice. Cover tightly with aluminum foil and bake in 350°F (180°C) oven for 1 hour.

Serves 6

Artichokes with Rice

From northern Italy comes this terrific dish that could be the scrumptious feature of an elegant luncheon.

1 lb (450 g) fresh artichoke hearts
18 fl oz (500 ml) water
18 fl oz (500 ml) dry white wine
8 tablespoons vegetable oil
12 oz (350 g) rice
salt and pepper to taste

1. Prepare artichoke hearts by pulling away the small leaves and trimming the stem. Then cut away the tough end parts of the leaves. Bend the leaves back and cut away and discard the tiny inner spiky leaves and the choke, being careful not to break the artichoke bottom or heart. Boil the hearts for about 10 minutes and set aside.
2. In a saucepan, Bring water and wine to a boil.
3. In another pan, heat 4 tablespoons of the oil and add the rice. Stir until well coated. Then pour in the water and wine mixture. Add salt and pepper. Cook on very low heat until rice is tender but firm. There should be some liquid left.
4. Cut the artichoke hearts into slices and fry them in the remaining oil, stirring, until lightly browned. Drain off the oil. Mix the artichokes with the rice and serve.

Serves 4

Asparagus

ASPARAGUS

This luxury vegetable with a luxurious taste has been cultivated since Roman times when, it is recorded, Julius Caesar ate it simply with melted butter.

In addition to their intense and rich flavour, asparagus provides vitamins A, B2, C, K, as well as potassium, iron and calcium.

The relatively short growing season lasts from late spring to early summer. Growing methods vary, but English and American asparagus are mostly grown above ground and produce green spears. On the continent, they are often grown under mounds of soil to produce white stalks.

To prepare, cut off the hard bottom of the stalk and trim any scars. An asparagus kettle, which allows spears to stand up in a wire basket, with tips pointing upwards, provides the ideal cooking method as the stalks take longer to cook than the tips. To boil asparagus, place spears in a saucepan of boiling water and simmer until just tender, about 5-6 minutes. Be careful not to overcook. Of course, there are many other simple methods, such as roasting them in a little olive oil.

RECIPES for ASPARAGUS

SOUPS
Asparagus Potato Soup 18
Cream of Asparagus Soup 19

APPETIZERS AND SALADS
Asparagus with Butter or Hollandaise 20
Asparagus with Vinaigrette 21

ACCOMPANIMENTS
Sautéed Asparagus 22
Baked Asparagus 23
Asparagus and Sour Cream Casserole 24
Asparagus with Rice 25
Asparagus Polonaise 26

Asparagus Potato Soup

*A variation on the familiar vichyssoise theme, this soup is
delicious either hot or cold.*

1 lb (450 g) asparagus
1 lb (450 g) potatoes, peeled and diced
1 small onion
3 sprigs parsley
24 fl oz (700 ml or 3 cups) water
salt
1 bouillon cube or 1 teaspoon chicken soup mix

1. Cut off and discard tough lower ends of the asparagus
   stalks. Wash and cut into shorter lengths.
2. Place in a saucepan together with all the other
   ingredients. Bring to a boil, then simmer covered until
   vegetables are tender, about 15 minutes.
3. Purée in a food processor or blender.
4. Refrigerate and serve cold. Or reheat and serve hot. If
   frozen, defrost and heat before serving.

Serves 6-8

Cream of Asparagus Soup

Another superlative soup, which is fantastic either hot or cold.

2 lbs (900 g) asparagus
4 large onions, chopped
8 tablespoons butter
64 fl oz (almost 2 litres or 8 cups) chicken stock
salt and freshly ground black pepper to taste
4 fl oz (100 ml or ½ cup) heavy cream (for cold soup)

1. Trim the tips from the asparagus and set them aside. Remove the woody ends from the bottoms of the asparagus spears. Chop spears into ½-inch (1.5 cm) pieces.
2. Melt the butter in a large pot and add the onions. Simmer, stirring frequently, until soft and golden, about 25 minutes.
3. Add chicken stock and bring to a boil. Then add the asparagus pieces to the stock. Cover, reduce heat, and simmer until asparagus is very soft, about 45 minutes.
4. Process the contents of the pot in a food processor. Return the purée to the pot. Add the reserved asparagus tips, and simmer until they are tender but still firm, about 5-10 minutes. Season with salt and pepper and serve hot.
6. If serving the soup cold, remove pot from heat and allow to cool. Stir in the cream and refrigerate. Serve very cold.

Serves 8-10

Asparagus with Butter or Hollandaise

Asparagus with butter is perhaps the easiest and most popular way of cooking and serving this elegant vegetable.

Asparagus:
3-4 asparagus spears per person, depending on size
butter

1. Wash the asparagus and cut off the tough ends of the stalks. Stand the stalks up in an asparagus or other deep kettle and add boiling salted water to a depth of two inches (5 cm). Cover with a lid and cook until just tender, about 12 minutes.
2. Drain and serve with melted butter or Hollandaise sauce.

Hollandaise sauce:
3 egg yolks
1 tablespoon cold water
4 oz (100 g or ½ cup) soft butter
¼ teaspoon salt
½-1 teaspoon lemon juice

1. Combine egg yolks and water in top of a double boiler and beat with a whisk over hot (not boiling) water until fluffy.
2. Add a few spoonfuls of butter at a time to the mixture and beat continually until butter has melted and sauce starts to thicken. Keep stirring as you add the butter, but be sure that the water in the bottom never boils.
3. Add salt and lemon juice. Serve with asparagus.

Asparagus with Vinaigrette

Here's another simple way of serving this elegant vegetable as a starter.

Asparagus:
3-4 asparagus spears per person, depending on size

1. Cut off the woody ends of the stems, rinse the spears, and drop them into boiling water. Cook uncovered from 8 to 14 minutes, until tender and done, testing with a prong. As cooking time depends on thickness of stalks, it's up to you.
2. When they are done—be careful not to overcook—put the asparagus in cold water to stop the cooking and to retain the bright green color. Drain and pat dry. Cover and refrigerate until ready.

Vinaigrette:
1 tablespoon Dijon mustard
4 tablespoons red wine vinegar
1 teaspoon sugar
½ teaspoon salt
½ teaspoon freshly ground black pepper
chopped parsley
4 fl oz (100ml or ½ cup) olive oil

1. In a bowl, whisk together first six ingredients.
2. Add olive oil slowly and continue to whisk until mixture is thickened.
3. Serve in a sauce boat with the asparagus.

Sautéed Asparagus

This simple accompaniment is a welcome treat and a change from the more usual vegetables.

1 lb (450 g) fresh asparagus
2 tablespoons olive oil
1-2 cloves garlic, minced

1. Cut off the tough portions of the lower stalks. Cut the asparagus diagonally into 1½ inch (3.8 cm) pieces.
2. Heat the oil in a large frying pan. Add the garlic and cook until it starts to color. Add the asparagus
3. Sauté the asparagus over medium heat, covered, stirring several times until the asparagus is cooked but still crisp, about 5-8 minutes.

Serves 4

Baked Asparagus

Prepare this asparagus dish in advance and pop it into the oven at the scheduled time.

1 lb (450 g) asparagus
2 tablespoons oil
2 tablespoons chopped fresh parsley
1 teaspoon chopped fresh dill
salt and pepper to taste
dash garlic powder

1. Cut off the lower tough ends of the asparagus stalks and discard them.
2. Cover the bottom of an 8-inch (20 cm) square baking dish with the oil. Place the asparagus spears in the dish and coat them with the oil.
3. Sprinkle with herbs and salt and pepper.
4. When ready, cover and bake in a 375°F (190°C) oven for 20-25 minutes.

Serves 4

Asparagus and Sour Cream Casserole

Another easy asparagus dish to add to your repertoire.

2½ lbs (1.2 kg) asparagus
salt and pepper to taste
8 fl oz (225 ml or 1 cup) sour cream
3 oz (75 g) bread crumbs
3 tablespoons melted butter

1. Cut the asparagus diagonally into 1½ inch (3.8 cm) pieces. Cook until just tender.
2. Place the drained asparagus in a greased casserole and sprinkle with salt and pepper. Stir in the sour cream.
3. Top with fresh bread crumbs which have been mixed with melted butter.
4. Bake in an oven preheated to 350°F (180°C) for 30 minutes or until top is brown.

Serves 6

Asparagus with Rice

Use hard, non-processed cheese to top this wonderful asparagus and rice combination.

2½ lbs (1.2 kg) asparagus
4 fl oz (100 ml or ½ cup) dry white wine
8 oz (225 g) raw rice
salt and pepper to taste
1½ oz (35 g or ½ cup) grated Parmesan cheese
1½ oz (35 g or ½ cup) Gruyere cheese, grated
6 tablespoons butter

1. Cook the asparagus until tender. Drain, reserving 1 cup (8 fl oz or 225 ml) cooking liquid.
2. Cook the rice in the reserved cooking liquid and the wine. Season with salt and pepper.
3. Place the rice and asparagus in layers in a shallow buttered dish. Sprinkle with the cheeses and dot with butter.
4. Place under grill or broiler until cheese has melted and top is brown.

Serves 6

Asparagus Polonaise

Polonaise means that the vegetable is sprinkled with buttered bread crumbs and sieved egg.

2 lbs (900 g) asparagus, cooked
6 tablespoons butter
3 tablespoons fine bread crumbs
1 hard-boiled egg, sieved
chopped parsley

1. Melt the butter in a saucepan and add the bread crumbs. Sauté until lightly browned.
2. Sprinkle the crumbs and butter over the hot, freshly-cooked asparagus. Then sprinkle with the sieved egg and chopped parsley.

Serves 4

Broccoli

BROCCOLI

This vegetable is a member of the massive cabbage family. Calabrese is the vegetable that we today commonly call broccoli, with large dark green flowerheads on the ends of stalks. It takes its name from Calabria, the province where this variety was first developed. Purple sprouting broccoli, the original variety, has long thin stalks and small flower-heads that are normally purple but can be green or white.

The Romans cooked purple sprouting broccoli in wine and served it with sauces. Still a popular vegetable in Italy, it is often served with pasta in a garlic and tomato sauce—or cooked in the oven with anchovies and onions.

Both varieties may be served simply with butter and lemon juice. They may also be served with a Hollandaise or Bearnaise sauce as an accompaniment. They are excellent when stir-fried.

Another variety called broccoli raab or rape has more stems and leaves and a more bitter but delicious taste. It can be used in any broccoli recipe.

It is a close relative to cauliflower and both vegetables can be used interchangeably in recipes.

This versatile and popular vegetable is delicious raw in salad, ideal in soup, great in casseroles, and excellent with pasta and cheese sauce.

This is a cool-weather crop with two seasons—early June through mid July and early September to late October.

RECIPES for BROCCOLI

APPETIZER
Broccoli Dip 30

SOUPS
Cold Broccoli Soup 31
Cream of Broccoli Soup 32

SALADS
Broccoli and Onion Salad 33
Broccoli Pasta Salad 34

ACCOMPANIMENTS
Broccoli Amandine 35
Broccoli and Mushrooms 36
Orange Broccoli 37
Sesame Broccoli 38
Braised Broccoli with Wine 39
Puréed Broccoli 40

MAIN COURSES
Broccoli and Pasta 41
Broccoli Baked Turkey 42

Broccoli Dip

A good starter to serve with crackers or raw vegetables.

1 large head (3 cups) cooked and coarsely chopped broccoli
4 oz (100 g or ½ cup) plain yogurt
3 tablespoons mayonnaise
3 oz (75 g) cream cheese
1 tablespoon lemon juice
2 tablespoons minced onion
1 garlic clove, minced
¼ teaspoon salt
dash of Tabasco or chili sauce (or to taste)

1. Steam the broccoli. Drain well and chop.
2. Place all ingredients in a blender or food processor. Process until the ingredients are well blended but not puréed.
3. Chill before serving.

Cold Broccoli Soup

*Among the myriad recipes for cream of broccoli soup is
this refreshing summertime treat.*

1 medium onion, sliced
1 medium carrot, sliced
1 small stalk celery with leaves, sliced
1 clove garlic, chopped
4 fl oz (100 ml or ½ cup) water
1 head broccoli (about 2 cups), cooked and coarsely
  chopped
1 teaspoon salt (or less)
pinch of cayenne pepper
2 oz (50 g or ¼ cup) cooked macaroni
8 fl oz (225 ml or 1 cup) chicken stock
4 fl oz (100 ml or ½ cup) cream
sour cream or creme fraiche

1. In a covered saucepan, simmer onion, carrot, celery,
   garlic, and water for 10 minutes.
2. Remove contents to an electric blender or food
   processor. Add broccoli, salt and cayenne and macaroni
   and process on high. Remove cover and, with motor still
   running, add the stock and the cream.
3. Chill. Serve with a dollop of sour cream on top.

Serves 6

Cream of Broccoli Soup

Actually, you can use an equivalent amount of another vegetable such as cauliflower, carrots, or turnips to make a cream of vegetable soup. Basically, you need only cook the vegetable you choose with good flavorings until it is done. Then purée it and reheat it with cream.

about 1 lb (450 g) broccoli, trimmed and cut up
4 oz (100 g or ½ cup) rice
32 fl oz (900 ml or 4 cups) chicken or vegetable stock
salt and pepper to taste
4-8 oz (100-225 ml) cream
fresh chopped parsley or chives for garnish

1. Combine the broccoli, rice and stock in a large saucepan on medium-high heat. Bring to a boil, then lower the heat and cook until broccoli is tender, about 15 minutes.
2. Purée in a blender or food processor. You may prepare the soup in advance up to this point. Just cover and refrigerate for up to 2 days, then reheat before proceeding.
3. Return to the pot and reheat over medium-low heat. Season with salt and freshly ground pepper. Add the cream. Heat through. Garnish and serve.

Serves 4

Broccoli and Onion Salad

This is an attractive salad that is very easy to prepare and very good to eat.

1 bunch fresh broccoli
1 medium red Spanish onion, cut into very thin slices
4 fl oz (100 ml or ½ cup) French dressing

1. Remove the leaves from the broccoli. Cut off any tough part of the stalk and cut large stalks in half. Cook in boiling salted water, uncovered, until just tender, about 10 minutes. Drain.
2. Place the warm broccoli in a shallow serving dish. Cover with the thinly sliced onion. Pour the dressing over all. Chill and serve.

Serves 6-8

Broccoli Pasta Salad

This unusual pasta salad may also serve four people when used as a main dish. Just add a tossed salad for a pleasant and refreshing meal.

1 head broccoli (about 2 cups), cut into flowerets
10 oz (275 g) snow peas, cut into ½ inch (1.2 cm) pieces
8 oz (225 g) pasta (spirals, macaroni, or any shape)
6 oz 175 ml) plain nonfat yogurt
2 fl oz (50 ml or ¼ cup) milk
2 teaspoons mayonnaise
3 tablespoons grated Parmesan cheese
1 teaspoon Dijon mustard
½ teaspoon dill weed
⅛ teaspoon garlic powder
pinch of pepper (or to taste)
10 small pitted green olives, chopped
1 salad pepper
2 green onions, chopped (green part only)

1. Place broccoli and snow peas in a colander.
2. Cook pasta according to directions and pour the cooking water into colander over the vegetables to slightly cook the vegetables. Then rinse under cold water and drain.
3. Combine remaining ingredients in a large serving bowl and mix well. Add pasta and vegetables. Toss well.
4. Chill several hours or overnight to allow flavors to blend.

Serves 6-8

Broccoli Amandine

Almonds and butter—what a good way to add variety to broccoli.

large bunch broccoli (about 1½ lbs or 700 g)
4 oz (100 g) butter, melted
lemon juice to taste
2 oz (50 g) coarsely chopped toasted almonds

1. Wash broccoli well. Cut off and discard large coarse leaves and tough lower parts of stalk. Cook until just tender.
2. Arrange in a heated serving dish.
3. Add lemon juice to the melted butter and add almonds. Sprinkle over the broccoli and serve.

Serves 4

Broccoli and Mushrooms

An easy way to make an excellent—and healthy—dish.

2 heads broccoli
1 tablespoon olive oil
2 cloves garlic, minced
8 oz (225 g) mushrooms, sliced
2 tablespoons water

1. Cut the broccoli into flowerets.
2. Heat the oil in a large frying pan. Add garlic, broccoli, and mushrooms. Stir for about a minute.
3. Add water, cover and cook over low heat until broccoli is just tender—about 5-10 minutes.

Serves 6

Orange Broccoli

Orange juice is added to this stir-fried broccoli side dish, a superb Oriental offering.

2 heads broccoli cut into flowerets (about 4 cups)
4 fl oz (100 ml or ½ cup) orange juice
1 tablespoon soy sauce
¼ teaspoon ground ginger
¼ teaspoon garlic powder
2 teaspoons honey
1 tablespoon cornstarch
1 tablespoon vegetable oil

1. Cut broccoli into flowerets.
2. In a small bowl combine orange juice, soy sauce, ginger, garlic powder, honey, and cornstarch. Mix until cornstarch is dissolved. Set aside.
3. Heat oil in a large frying pan over medium heat. Add broccoli and cook for about 2 minutes, stirring frequently, until broccoli is bright green.
4. Pour the orange juice mixture over the broccoli. Continue cooking and stirring for a few minutes, until broccoli is evenly coated and the sauce is thick and clear.

Serves 4

Sesame Broccoli

Here is a dish of broccoli that provides both heart-healthy and pleasurable eating.

2 heads broccoli, cut into flowerets
1 tablespoon soy sauce
1 tablespoons sesame oil
2 fl oz (50 ml or ¼ cup) dry sake or sherry
1-2 teaspoons honey
1 tablespoon sesame seeds, toasted

1. Mix together in a bowl the soy sauce, sesame oil, wine, and honey. Set the dressing aside.
2. Steam the cut-up broccoli until tender.
3. Pour the dressing mixture over the steamed broccoli and toss to mix.
4. Sprinkle sesame seeds over the broccoli and serve.

Serves 8

Braised Broccoli with Wine

This Italian preparation is also good served at room temperature.

1½ lbs (700 g) broccoli
3 tablespoons olive oil
3 anchovies, minced (optional)
1 clove garlic, minced
8 fl oz (225 ml or 1 cup) dry white wine
salt and pepper

1. Trim and cut up the broccoli.
2. Place oil in a large frying pan on medium heat. Add the anchovies and garlic. Cook and stir until the garlic begins to color, about 3 to 5 minutes.
3. Add the broccoli and continue to cook and stir for another 3 to 4 minutes.
4. Add the wine and allow it to bubble away for a minute or two. Cover and cook on medium-low heat for 2 or 3 minutes.
5. Uncover and cook on medium heat for about 5 minutes or until most of the wine has evaporated and broccoli is tender. Season to taste with salt and freshly ground black pepper.

Serves 4

Puréed Broccoli

Green and delicious, this purée goes well with most main courses.

2 bunches (about 5 lbs or 2.2 kg) broccoli
8 oz (225 g or 1 cup) crème fraîche
4 tablespoons sour cream
⅔ cup freshly grated Parmesan cheese
½ teaspoon freshly grated nutmeg
freshly ground black pepper
salt to taste
2 tablespoons butter

1. Trim and chop the broccoli, including the peeled stems. Leave whole 8 small flowerets. Cook the chopped broccoli and the whole flowerets in 4 quarts of boiling water until just tender, about 8 minutes.
2. Put aside the 8 whole flowerets and transfer the rest of the broccoli to a food processor. Add crème fraîche and purée thoroughly.
3. Turn the purée into a bowl and mix in the sour cream, Parmesan cheese, nutmeg, pepper and salt. Mix well.
4. Pile the mixture into an ovenproof serving dish and dot with butter. Bake in an oven preheated to 350°F (180°C) for about 25 minutes, until it is heated through.
5. Garnish with reserved flowerets and serve immediately.

Serves 6-8

Broccoli and Pasta

This flavorful and filling dish is a fine accompaniment but needs only a crusty baguette to turn it into a satisfying meal.

1 lb (450 g) broccoli (or more)
2 oz (50 g or ¼ cup) olive oil
1 clove garlic, minced
1 lb (450 g) pasta (elbow macaroni, ziti, penne, etc.)
salt and pepper
chopped fresh parsley for garnish

1. Trim the broccoli and divide it into small florets. Drop in a large pot of boiling salted water and cook until crisp-tender. Remove broccoli and set aside.
2. Place oil in a deep frying pan and sauté garlic in it over medium-low heat until it is golden.
3. Add the broccoli and cook over medium heat for just a few minutes, stirring and mashing until it is hot and soft.
4. Cook the pasta until it is nearly done. Drain, saving about a cup of the cooking liquid. Add the pasta to the pan and toss to mix it all together. Add salt and freshly ground pepper to taste, together with some of the pasta water to keep the mixture from drying out.
5. Garnish with chopped parsley and serve.

Serves 4

Broccoli Baked Turkey

What a good way to make a main course of broccoli while using up leftover turkey.

1 head broccoli
2 tablespoons butter
3 tablespoons plain white flour
10 fl oz (300 ml) chicken broth or stock
½ teaspoon salt
8 oz (225 g) mushrooms, sliced
about 1 lb (or 2 cups) cooked turkey breast, diced

1. Trim stems and leaves off broccoli. Separate the flowerets and steam them until they are just tender. Set aside.
2. Melt butter in a saucepan. Remove from heat and stir in the flour until it makes a smooth paste.
3. Return to low heat and mix in the chicken broth, stirring constantly until sauce is smooth and thick.
4. Add salt and mushrooms and mix together.
5. Grease a shallow baking pan with butter and place broccoli in pan. Arrange turkey over the broccoli. Pour mushroom sauce over both.
6. Bake uncovered in oven preheated to 375°F (190°C) for 15-25 minutes.

Serves 6

Brussels Sprouts

BRUSSELS SPROUTS

First cultivated in the Middle Ages in Flanders, Brussels sprouts are essentially miniature cabbages that grow in a row on a long, tough stalk.

Although closely related to cabbage, Brussels sprouts have a nutty flavor quite unlike cabbage. Indeed, they go well with certain nuts, especially sweet-flavored ones such as almonds

Brussels sprouts are a winter vegetable, harvested from September or October through early spring. The flavor is improved by frost. They should be small and hard with tightly wrapped leaves.

To prepare, trim and wash them before cooking. Remove the outer leaves and cut off the bottom of the stalk. Some people cut an X in the stem end for even or quicker cooking. In any case, do not overcook as they lose their flavor. Simmer in boiling water for about eight minutes until just tender. They are done when easily pierced with a skewer or thin-bladed knife. Or steam them for ten to twelve minutes. Cooking time varies, depending on size. To stir-fry, cut them in half or into three or four slices (depending on size), then fry in a little oil and butter. Delicious with onions and ginger!

RECIPES for BRUSSELS SPROUTS

APPETIZERS
Marinated Brussels Sprouts 46

ACCOMPANIMENTS

Marinated Brussels Sprouts

This unusual starter may be served with pre-prandial drinks.

1½ lbs (700 g) small Brussels sprouts
8 oz (225 g or 1 cup) sugar
6 fl oz (175 ml or ¾ cup) cider vinegar
1 teaspoon salt
½ teaspoon dry mustard
1 teaspoon oregano
⅛ teaspoon pepper

1. Cook Brussels sprouts, being careful not to overcook. Place them in a shallow dish.
2. Combine remaining ingredients and pour mixture over the Brussels sprouts. Cover and allow to marinate in refrigerator overnight.
3. Drain. Serve with cocktail picks.

about 20 servings

Brussels Sprouts Amandine

The nutty flavor of sprouts goes particularly well with almonds.

1 lb (450 g) Brussels sprouts
3 tablespoons butter
4-5 tablespoons blanched, slivered almonds

1. Wash, trim, and cook the Brussels sprouts. Drain them and cut them in half.
2. Melt the butter in a large frying pan. Add the almonds and sauté them over medium heat until lightly browned. Add the halved Brussels sprouts and sauté together with almonds for about 1 minute.

Serves 4

Brussels Sprouts with Caraway Seeds

An original way to serve sprouts.

1½ lbs (700 g) Brussels sprouts
chicken stock
3 tablespoons butter
salt and pepper to taste
2 teaspoons whole caraway seeds

1. Wash and trim the Brussels sprouts.
2. Pour chicken stock into a saucepan to reach a depth of one inch (2.5 cm) and bring to a boil. Add the sprouts and return to the boil. Lower heat and simmer for three minutes uncovered. Then cover and cook until just tender.
3. Drain if necessary. Mix in remaining ingredients and serve.

Serves 6

Brussels Sprouts with Tomato and Onion

This is an imaginative way to vary this excellent winter vegetable.

1 lb (450 g) small Brussels sprouts
3 tablespoons butter
1 medium onion, chopped
2-3 tomatoes, peeled and coarsely chopped
salt and pepper
1 tablespoon grated Parmesan cheese (optional)

1. Cook the Brussels sprouts until tender. Remove from heat, drain, and cut each sprout in half.
2. Melt butter in a saucepan. Add the onion and cook until soft. Add tomatoes, sprouts, and salt and pepper to taste. Cook for 2-3 minutes over medium heat or until the tomatoes are heated through.
3. Sprinkle with Parmesan cheese and serve.

Serves 4

Baked Brussels Sprouts

*Baked together with chestnuts, this vegetable dish is a
good choice for a dinner party as it needs no attention
once it is ready for the oven.*

1 lb (450 g) Brussels sprouts
4 oz (110 g) carrot, chopped
1 small onion, chopped
6 oz (175 g) fresh chestnuts
15 fl oz (450 ml) vegetable stock or water
2 oz (50 g) butter
1 oz (25 g) wholewheat flour
salt and pepper to taste
3 slices lemon

1. Clean sprouts and cut them in half.
2. Chop carrot and onion and cook them in stock, in a
   saucepan, for about 10 minutes. During the last few
   minutes of cooking add sprouts.
3. Transfer contents of pan (vegetables and stock) into an
   ovenproof dish or casserole. Add the chestnuts.
4. Mix butter with the flour and stir into the vegetables.
   Bring mixture to a boil. Season with salt and pepper.
   Arrange lemon slices within the vegetables.
5. Cover and keep until ready to heat and serve.
6. Bake in 350°F (180°C) oven for about 30 minutes.

Serves 4-6

Lemon-Dill Brussels Sprouts

An easy accompaniment that goes especially well with fish.

1 lb (450 g) Brussels sprouts
1 tablespoon butter
2 tablespoons lemon juice
2 teaspoons dill weed
salt and pepper

1. Cook Brussels sprouts until barely tender.
2. Heat butter in saucepan. Stir in lemon juice and dill Add the cooked Brussels sprouts to the saucepan. Season with salt and pepper to taste.

Serves 4

Brussels Sprouts with Water Chestnuts

The water chestnuts add a crunchy note to this flavorful way of preparing sprouts.

1-2 tablespoons olive oil
1 lb (500 g) Brussels sprouts
grated rind of 1 orange
2 oz (50 g) butter
2 teaspoons wholegrain mustard
1 tin (about 4 oz or 115 g) water chestnuts
salt and pepper

1. Wash and trim sprouts. Cut them in half.
2. Heat the oil in a pan and add grated orange rind. Then add butter, mustard and sprouts.
3. Cook over medium heat for about 5 minutes, stirring frequently, until sprouts are crisp.
4. Drain the water chestnuts chop them, and stir them into the sprouts. Cook for 3-4 minutes until they are heated through and the sprouts have a golden colour.
5. Add salt and freshly ground black pepper to taste and serve.

Serves 4

Brussels Sprouts au Gratin

*Try this recipe for variety and appeal. It can be prepared
the night before, leaving very little preparation before
serving.*

1 lb (450 g) Brussels sprouts
1 tablespoon butter
1 tablespoon flour
4 fl oz (125 ml or ½ cup) chicken broth
2 fl oz (50 ml or ¼ cup) double or heavy cream
1 oz (25 g) grated Swiss or Parmesan cheese
buttered crumbs

1. Cook the Brussels sprouts until they are just tender and
   can be pierced with a skewer or fork. Transfer them to a
   greased casserole.
2. Melt butter in a saucepan, stir in flour, and cook until
   thickened. Add broth gradually, stirring constantly. Add
   cream. Cook, stirring until the mixture is thick and
   smooth. Then stir in grated cheese.
3. Pour sauce into casserole over the Brussels sprouts. Top
   with buttered crumbs and bake in an oven preheated to
   350°F (180°C) for 15 minutes.

Serves 4

Purée of Brussels Sprouts

Here is a side dish that is surprisingly delicious. Delicately flavored and beautifully green, it goes well with game or fowl, roast beef or lamb. This recipe lists ingredients, but the quantities are up to you.

Brussels sprouts
cream
butter
salt and pepper
freshly ground nutmeg

1. Cook the Brussels sprouts in a small amount of water for as short a time as possible. (They may be undercooked.)
2. Process them with a little cream in an electric blender or food processor until you have a purée.
3. When you are ready to serve, reheat the purée with a little more cream and a little butter. Season with salt and freshly ground black pepper and some freshly ground nutmeg.

Cabbage

CABBAGE

The many varieties of cabbages allow for a year-round supply. Cabbage is a popular winter vegetable that has almost always and everywhere symbolized peasant food. But it has great versatility and, as a member of the cruciferous family of vegetables, has important nutritional benefits including vitamins K and C.

The ancient Greeks and Romans enjoyed this vegetable, but it is not known whether it was the same variety as today's round variety. Cabbage was abundant and basic in the Dark Ages.

Cabbage is a brassica with many varieties: savoy cabbage (curly leaves and mild flavor), spring greens (loose heads and pale yellow-green head), green cabbage (loose-leafed with slightly pointed head), red cabbage (firm leaves with beautiful color that fades during cooking unless a little vinegar is added to water), white cabbage (smooth and firm light green leaves, also called Dutch cabbage), and Napa or Chinese cabbage (a romaine-like variety). Bok choy, a favorite in Chinese cooking, is another welcome member of the cabbage family.

Cabbage is excellent both for salads and for cooking. Heads should be firm. To shred, cut cabbage into quarters through the core, cut away the core, and slice evenly. Proper cooking will produce a fragrant aroma and sweet flavor. Methods include boiling, stuffing, stir frying, making soups or casseroles.

RECIPES for CABBAGE

Cabbage and Potato Soup

This North European staple makes a delicious soup that is even better the next day. Serve with dark, crusty bread.

1 small cabbage (about 1½ lbs or 700 g), coarsley shredded
2 medium potatoes, cut into cubes
4 tablespoons butter
1 large onion, chopped
2-3 tomatoes, peeled, seeded, and roughly chopped
40 fl oz (1.2 litres or 5 cups) chicken stock or water
½ teaspoon dried thyme
salt and freshly ground pepper
1-2 tablespoons lemon juice

1. Core and shred the cabbage. Peel and cut potatoes—waxy ones are best—into cubes.
2. Melt butter in a large saucepan on medium heat. Add cabbage, potatoes, onions, and tomatoes. You may substitute a can of plum tomatoes with the liquid.) Add the stock or water and the thyme and seasonings.
3. Bring to a boil, then reduce heat to low and simmer, stirring occasionally, for about 30-45 minutes, until potatoes and cabbage are tender and tomatoes have fallen apart. Add lemon juice and adjust seasonings. Serve hot.

Serves 6-8

Asian Style Cabbage Soup

Use Savoy cabbage if possible for this really delicious Asian-style soup, which may be prepared in advance and refrigerated for up to 2 days before serving. Just reheat when ready and add lime juice.

small head (about 1½ lbs (700 g) cabbage
3 tablespoons peanut or vegetable oil
1 large onion, sliced
salt and pepper to taste
1 tablespoon fresh ginger, minced
2 tablespoons soy sauce
40 fl oz (1.2 litres or 5 cups) chicken stock or water
freshly squeezed lime juice

1. Core and shred the cabbage.
2. Place oil in a large saucepan on medium heat. Add the cabbage, onion, salt and pepper. Cook and stir until vegetables are tender. Reduce heat and continue cooking for another 20 minutes.
3. Stir in the ginger. Cook and stir for 1 minute. Add the soy sauce and stock or water. Continue to cook, stirring occasionally, for about 15 minutes.
4. Just before serving the hot soup, add a squeeze of lime juice and adjust seasonings.

Serves 4

Coleslaw with Caraway

The addition of caraway to coleslaw enhances the cabbage flavor enormously.

1 large head cabbage
1 small onion, finely chopped
salt and pepper to taste
lemon juice, to taste
6 oz (175 ml or ¾ cup) mayonnaise
1 tablespoon caraway seeds

1. Remove core and outer leaves from cabbage and discard. Chop cabbage into shreds or cubes and mix in the chopped onion, salt and freshly ground black pepper, and lemon juice.
2. Add mayonnaise and caraway seeds and blend mixture well. Adjust the seasonings and chill.

Serves 8

Spicy Coleslaw

Try this for a healthier and more interesting variation of the usual and traditional coleslaw.

head of green or Savoy cabbage
2 red peppers, diced
2-3 green onions, diced
2 tablespoons Dijon mustard
2 tablespoons balsamic vinegar
1 tablespoon sugar
4 fl oz (125 ml or ½ cup) olive or peanut oil
salt and freshly ground pepper
3-4 tablespoon chopped fresh parsley

1. Core and shred the cabbage. Combine with peppers and green onions.
2. Combine the dressing ingredients. Add to cabbage and toss. Season with salt and pepper.
3. Refrigerate until ready to serve. Allow to stand for several hours or overnight to give the flavors a chance to blend.
4. Toss with parsley just before serving.

Serves 6-8

Pineapple Coleslaw

This delicious version makes a change from standard coleslaw. As with most coleslaws, it tastes best when made a day ahead.

1 head cabbage, finely shredded
1 large carrot, finely shredded
½ green pepper, finely chopped
1 small can crushed pineapple (unsweetened), undrained
2 tablespoons plus 2 teaspoons mayonnaise
1 tablespoon wine vinegar
1 teaspoon Dijon mustard
1 tablespoon sugar
salt and pepper

1. Combine cabbage, carrots, green pepper, and pineapple in a large bowl.
2. Blend remaining ingredients in a small bowl and add to cabbage mixture. Mix well.
3. Chill several hours or overnight. Stir before serving.

Serves 6-8

Asian Cabbage Slaw

*Here is a refreshing salad which could make a welcome
change from the usual coleslaws. It can be kept covered
and refrigerated for three to four days.*

1 medium-large head cabbage, finely shredded
1-2 carrots, grated
½ red or green pepper, diced or julienned

Dressing:
2 tablespoons vegetable oil
2 tablespoons rice vinegar
1 tablespoon soy sauce
2 teaspoons brown sugar
½ teaspoon grated fresh ginger root
dash of chili oil or hot pepper sauce (optional)

3-4 tablespoons chopped peanuts or
1 tablespoon toasted sesame seeds (optional)

1. In a large serving bowl, combine the cabbage, carrots,
   and peppers.
2. In another bowl, whisk together the oil, vinegar, soy
   sauce, brown sugar, ginger, and chili oil or pepper sauce.
3. Pour the dressing over the cabbage mixture and mix
   well. Allow to marinate for at least an hour or so.
4. Toss again just before serving. Add the chopped peanuts
   or sesame seeds, if desired.

Serves 4-6

Cabbage a la Russe

A horseradish cream dressing makes this cabbage salad very special.

1 small head white cabbage, finely shredded
2½ teaspoons sugar
salt and freshly ground black pepper to taste
cayenne pepper to taste
12 prunes
half a green pepper, cut into strips
4 fl oz (100 ml) heavy or whipping cream
1 fl oz (25 ml) white wine vinegar
1½ tablespoons grated horseradish
1 teaspoon finely chopped or grated onion

1. Shred the cabbage and place in a large bowl. Add the sugar, salt and pepper and toss well. Add cayenne pepper and toss again.
2. Plump the prunes in very hot water and remove the pits. Cut into narrow strips and add to cabbage together with green pepper. Mix well.
3. Make the dressing by beating the cream until stiff. Gradually beat in the wine vinegar. Add the horseradish and onion and mix well. Mix dressing into salad and chill.

6 servings

Buttered Cabbage

Butter enhances this basic and simple way of preparing cabbage.

1 head cabbage
water or stock, as needed
salt and freshly ground black pepper
butter, as desired

1. Remove and discard discolored outer leaves. Wash, core and cut into wedges or shreds.
2. Cook in small amount of boiling water or stock until tender. Drain well.
3. Season with salt and pepper. Add melted butter and serve.

Serves 4-6

Fried Cabbage with Grainy Mustard

Forget that awful overcooked and smelly cabbage when you prepare and eat the delicious winter vegetable produced by this recipe.

half a large cabbage or one small cabbage
3 oz (75 g) butter
2 tablespoons grainy mustard
salt and freshly ground black pepper

1. Shred the cabbage finely.
2. Melt butter in a shallow pan and stir the mustard into it. Add the cabbage.
3. Cook over a gentle heat, stirring occasionally, for up to 30 minutes, depending on how crunchy you want it.

Serves 4-6

Stir-Fried Cabbage

Pak choy is the best cabbage to stir-fry, although you can use other varieties. You can also vary this recipe by adding mushrooms with the pak choy or cabbage, or by substituting white wine for the stock.

2 lbs (900 g) pak choy
2 tablespoons peanut or vegetable oil
2-3 cloves garlic, minced
1 tablespoon minced fresh ginger
2 green onions or scallions
8 fl oz (225 ml or 1 cup) chicken stock
1 tablespoon soy sauce
salt and pepper (if necessary)

1. Cut pak choy into 1-inch (2.5 cm) sections.
2. Heat the oil in a large frying pan or wok. Add the garlic, ginger and green onions. Cook and stir for a few seconds, then add the cabbage and turn the heat to high.
3. Cook and stir for another 3 minutes. Add the stock. Continue cooking and stirring until liquid evaporates and the cabbage is tender, about 5 minutes.
4. Add soy sauce. Remove from heat. Season with salt and pepper if needed. Serve.

Serves 4-6

Braised Cabbage with Nutmeg

Any cabbage—green, white, Savoy, pak choy—may be braised, and adding a spice such as nutmeg produces a particularly lovely dish.

1 head cabbage, about 1½ lbs (700 g)
1 tablespoon olive oil
salt and pepper
4 fl oz (125 ml or ½ cup) white wine
1 teaspoon brown sugar
¼ teaspoon freshly grated nutmeg

1. Trim and shred the cabbage.
2. Place oil in deep frying pan over medium heat and add the cabbage. Cook and stir until it begins to brown, about 5 minutes.
3. Add salt and pepper. Add wine and let it bubble away for a minute or so. Add the sugar and nutmeg.
4. Cover and simmer until tender, about 15 minutes.

Serves 4

:

Cabbage Curry

One ingredient of this unusual and tasty East Indian dish is masala; this mixture of ground black peppercorns, cardamom, caraway, cinnamon, cloves, and coriander is available at Indian specialty shops.

1 medium head cabbage (about 2 lbs or 1 kg)
1 medium onion, chopped
1 tablespoon butter
2 teaspoons salt
1 teaspoon ground turmeric
½ teaspoon chili powder (optional)
1 teaspoon masala

1. Discard outer leaves and slice cabbage thinly.
2. Sauté onion in butter until lightly browned. Mix in salt, turmeric, and chili powder. Add cabbage and cook over medium heat, without stirring, for 15 minutes. Then stir gently.
3. Continue to cook, partially covered, until the cabbage is cooked through. Continue to stir gently to keep from sticking.
4. Add the masala and cook, stirring, for another minute or two. The curry should be very dry. Serve hot.

Serves 6

Cabbage with Caraway Seeds and Wine

Although not usually thought of as company fare, cabbage can be a culinary delight, especially with caraway seeds as the perfect partner. This dish goes extremely well with goose, duck, or roast chicken.

1 head cabbage, finely sliced
2 oz (50 g) butter
1 teaspoon olive oil
2 onions, sliced
1 tablespoon flour
1 glass white wine (red if using red cabbage)
salt and freshly ground black pepper to taste
2 teaspoons caraway seeds
1 tablespoon wine vinegar
1 tablespoon brown sugar
1 large apple

1. Remove outer leaves and core and cut cabbage into fine slices.
2. Heat butter and oil together in a large pan. Fry the onion in it until soft.
3. Mix the flour with the wine to make a thin paste and stir it into the onions. Mix in the sliced cabbage.
4. Add all the remaining ingredients except the apple and cook on low heat with lid on, stirring occasionally.
5. Add the apple, peeled and cut into 8 pieces. Continue to cook gently for another 15 minutes.

Serves 4-6

Brittany Cabbage

A little more effort goes into the preparation of this dish from Brittany.

1 medium-size head cabbage
16 fl oz (475 ml or 2 cups) beef stock
2 eggs, well beaten
6 fl oz (175 ml or ¾ cup) light cream
½ teaspoon salt
freshly ground black pepper to taste
nutmeg to taste
3 tablespoons olive oil
3 tablespoons tarragon vinegar
2 teaspoons sugar
paprika

1. Cut the cabbage into eight wedges. Cook in the stock until tender. Drain and keep warm.
2. In a bowl, mix the eggs, cream, salt, and pepper.
3. Heat the oil, vinegar and sugar in a saucepan and bring to boiling. While stirring, add to the egg mixture. Return to saucepan and cook on very low heat until thickened.
4. Remove core from cabbage and discard. Place cabbage in a warm bowl and pour sauce over it. Sprinkle with paprika. Let stand a few minutes before serving.

4 servings

Austrian Cabbage with Sour Cream

Sour cream and paprika are the typical ingredients of dishes belonging to the Austro-Hungarian period.

1 small white cabbage, about 1½ lbs (750 g)
1 small onion
4 tablespoons vegetable oil
juice of half a lemon
9 fl oz (250 ml) sour cream
1 egg
salt and freshly-ground black pepper
½ teaspoon paprika

1. Remove discolored outer leaves. Wash cabbage and cut into quarters. Cut out the core and shred the cabbage.
2. Peel onion and chop finely.
3. Heat butter in a pan over medium heat and cook the onion until it is soft and tender. Add cabbage and sauté until it is coated. Cook with lid on until cabbage is very soft, about 20 minutes. Add the lemon juice. Season to taste with salt and pepper and paprika.
4. Beat the egg with the sour cream and pour over cabbage. Stir over low heat for 6-8 minutes, until the cream thickens a little, but do now allow to boil.
5. Serve immediately.

Serves 4-6

King Cabbage

Cabbage, topped with onions and melted cheese, is a vegetable dish fit for royalty.

1 small cabbage (1 lb or 450 g), sliced ½ inch (1.2 cm) thick
2 teaspoons sugar
1 teaspoon caraway seeds
1 medium onion, thinly sliced
salt and pepper to taste
2 oz (50 g) mozzarella cheese (or Swiss)

1. Place cabbage slices in the bottom of a lightly oiled 8-inch (20.3) cm) square baking dish.
2. Sprinkle evenly with *half* of the sugar and *half* the caraway seeds.
3. Place onion slices over the cabbage. Sprinkle with remaining sugar and caraway seeds. Sprinkle with salt and freshly ground pepper to taste.
4. Cover and bake in oven preheated to 350°F (180°C). for 1 hour.
5. Uncover and sprinkle with finely slivered or grated cheese. Return to oven for 5 minutes to melt cheese.

Serves 4

New England Vegetarian Dinner

*This superb dish may be served over cooked brown rice.
Or it may be spooned into bowls and served with thick,
crusty bread to make a satisfying meal. Not limited to New
England, it even transfers well to Old England.*

1 medium-large head cabbage, coarsely chopped
3 medium potatoes, cut into 1-inch cubes
3-4 carrots, cut into ½-inch (1.2 cm) slices
3-4 leeks, white part only, cut into ½-inch (1.2 cm) slices
1 teaspoon caraway seeds
2 teaspoons paprika
½ teaspoon garlic powder
salt and pepper to taste
16 fl oz (450 ml or 2 cups) water
6 oz (175 g) Cheddar cheese, shredded

1. Place cabbage, potatoes, carrots, and leeks in a large
   Dutch oven. Sprinkle spices over the vegetables and
   mix well. Add water.
2. Bring to a boil over medium heat, stirring occasionally.
   Cover, reduce heat, and simmer 30 minutes.
3. Spread cheese evenly over cooked vegetables. Place in
   oven preheated to 350°F (180°C) and bake, covered, for
   25 minutes.

Serves 6-8

Courgettes or Zucchini

COURGETTES or ZUCCHINI

Courgettes and zucchini are exactly the same thing. They are mainly called zucchini by Italians and Americans, while the French and British refer to them as courgettes. I use the terms interchangeably in this book. Marrows, incidentally, are overgrown zucchini (courgettes).

This is a crop that is easy to grow. Even the person who does not have a garden can grow zucchini at home, in a tub on the balcony or in some outdoor space. Freshly picked when they are still small, zucchini are remarkably good. You may become addicted to this wonderful and versatile vegetable.

The great thing about harvesting an abundant crop is the infinite variety of ways in which to use it. Perhaps the most versatile of all vegetables, this prolific plant deserves a book of its own. The book exists: *What Will I Do With All Those Courgettes?* by Elaine Borish. I include here just a few sample recipes, unusual but easy, from that volume, which contains over 150 recipes.

RECIPES for COURGETTES OR ZUCCHINI

APPETIZER
Zucchini à la Grecque 78

SOUP
Zucchini and Mint Soup 79

SALAD
Zucchini Vinaigrette 80

ACCOMPANIMENT
Sicilian Style Sweet and Sour Zucchini 81

BREAD and CAKE
Zucchini Bread 82

Zucchini à la Grecque

This recipe is equally good eaten hot (as a vegetable accompaniment to a main course) or cold (as a first course, perhaps served on lettuce leaves).

5-6 tablespoons olive oil
2 large onions, thinly sliced
2 large cloves of garlic, crushed
8 small-medium zucchini, sliced into rounds
6 medium tomatoes, skinned, seeded and chopped
1 tablespoon lemon juice
1 tablespoon fresh chopped tarragon (or 1 teaspoon dried)
pinch of thyme
salt
freshly ground black pepper

1. Heat the oil in a frying pan. Sauté the onions until they are soft and transparent.
2. Add the garlic to the pan together with the sliced zucchini (about ½ inch or 1 cm thick) and cook for a few minutes.
3. Add the tomatoes and lemon juice.
4. Mix in tarragon, thyme, and salt and pepper to taste.
5. Simmer gently for about 45 minutes.

Serves 8

Zucchini and Mint Soup

Here's a sensational soup that can be served either hot or cold.

2 oz (50 g) butter
2 medium onions, chopped
2 lbs (900 g) zucchini, cut into chunks
24 oz (700 ml or 3 cups) chicken stock
2 handfuls of mint leaves
salt
freshly ground black pepper

1. In a large pot, melt the butter and add the chopped onions. Sauté over low heat until the onions are soft and translucent, about 10 minutes. Add the zucchini and cook for an additional 5 minutes.
2. Add the chicken stock and 1 handful of mint leaves.
3. Cover and simmer for 30 minutes. Cool
4. Blend the contents in a food processor together with the remaining handful of mint leaves.
5. Add more water if needed and season with salt and pepper.

Serves 6

Zucchini Vinaigrette

I make this for fancy picnics and large barbecue parties.

2 lbs (1 kg) small zucchini, cut into ¼-inch (.6 cm) slices
1 small medium red onion, chopped
1 teaspoon oregano or basil
2 oz (50 g) chopped parsley
6 fl oz (180 ml or ¾ cup) French dressing
1-2 cloves garlic, crushed

1. Cook zucchini in a large pot of boiling water for just 2 minutes. Drain immediately in a colander and rinse in cold water to stop the cooking process.
2. Place zucchini in a bowl and add onion, oregano and parsley.
3. Mix crushed garlic with the French dressing and pour over the zucchini.
4. Blend thoroughly and chill.

Serves 8

Sicilian Style Sweet and Sour Zucchini

The southern Italy version of sweet and sour zucchini.

2 lbs (1 kg) zucchini
2 large cloves garlic, crushed
3 tablespoons olive oil
3 tablespoons red wine vinegar
2 tablespoons water
1 oz (25 g) raisins or sultanas
1 oz (25 g) pine kernels
8 anchovy fillets
salt and freshly ground black pepper

1. Heat the oil in a large frying pan and sauté garlic. Add zucchini, cut into strips 2-3 inches (5.8 cm) long, and stir gently until they turn golden.
2. Add vinegar and water. Cover and simmer for 10-12 minutes.
3. Add raisins, pine kernels, and anchovies (rinsed of any salt or oil and chopped) and cook uncovered, until the liquid is reduced.
4. Add salt and pepper and stir to steep zucchini in the flavors of the sauce.

Serves 6

Zucchini Bread

As this recipe makes two loaves, keep one in the freezer for emergency use. You can also store chopped zucchini in measured quantities in the freezer, ready for baking in those off-season months when zucchini is not available from your garden.

3 eggs, beaten
4 oz (110 g or ½ cup sugar
5 oz (140 g) brown sugar
4 fl oz (120 ml or ½ cup) sunflower oil
3 teaspoons maple flavoring
2 coarsely chopped zucchini (2 cups, about 1 lb or 450g)
2 teaspoons baking soda
½ teaspoon baking powder
½ teaspoon salt
4 oz (110 g or ½ cup) wheat germ
20 oz (550 g or 2½ cups) flour
4 oz (110 g or ½ cup) walnuts, chopped
4-6 tablespoons sesame seeds

1. Beat eggs. Add sugars, oil and maple flavoring, and beat all together until thick and foamy. Stir in zucchini.
2. Add baking soda, baking powder, salt, wheat germ and flour. Mix well. Blend in the walnuts.
3. Turn batter into two greased 9 x 5 inch (23 x 13 cm) loaf pans. Sprinkle sesame seeds over tops.
4. Bake in preheated oven at 350°F (180°C) for 45-55 minutes or until a toothpick inserted into center comes out clean.

Yields 2 loaves, 12 slices each

Fennel

FENNEL

Another vegetable with a long history, fennel is said to have been cultivated by the ancient Egyptians, Greeks, and Romans. It has been popular for several centuries in Italy, where it is known as *finocchio*. Indeed, Italy produces some of the best recipes.

Pale green in color, this vegetable looks like a root, but it is actually the swollen stem. Bulbs should be small and tender, clean and white, with lively feathery leaves.

Like the herb and spice to which it is related, fennel has the flavor of anise. It is often served with fish dishes, as its distinctive taste goes particularly well with fish. It's also great with roast lamb or chicken—and so many other dishes. The edible leaves can be used in stocks (like the herb or spice) or used as a garnish.

Fennel can be eaten raw in salads and enjoyed for its celery-like crispness. Simply remove the first layer of skin if it is tough. Then cut downwards to slice into slivers or cut across the bulb for rings. Serve with vinaigrette.

RECIPES for FENNEL

APPETIZER
Fennel à la Grecque 86

SALADS
Fennel and Orange Salad 87
Fennel and Celeriac Salad 88

ACCOMPANIMENTS
Fennel au Gratin 89
Italian Fennel Casserole 90
Baked Fennel 91

LUNCHEON DISH
Ragout of Fennel and Green Beans 92

Fennel à la Grecque

This makes a refreshing first course for a summertime meal. Or it can be part of a mixed hors d'oeuvre. Partnered with thinly-sliced smoked raw Parma ham, it makes a delightful and substantial first course.

3 fennel bulbs (1 lb or 450 g)
15 fl oz (450 ml) water
2-3 tablespoons olive oil
juice of 1 lemon
½ teaspoon salt
12 black peppercorns
6 coriander seeds
6 sprigs parsley
1-2 shallots, finely chopped
small piece celery
parsley or fresh herbs for garnish

1. Cut fennel bulbs into halves or quarters.
2. Prepare the broth with all the ingredients except the fennel and the herbs for garnish. Bring to the boil, then lower heat and simmer for 10 minutes.
3. Add fennel bulbs and simmer for another 10 minutes.
4. Remove fennel to a serving dish. Boil the cooking liquid rapidly to reduce to about 3 tablespoons of liquid. Strain over the fennel and chill.
5. Sprinkle with fresh chopped herbs to garnish and serve.

Serves 4-6

Fennel and Orange Salad

The mild anise flavor of the fennel makes a pleasing and refreshing salad, which is also very attractive.

2 fennel bulbs
4 oranges
juice of 1 lemon
2 tablespoons olive oil
salt and pepper to taste

1. Slice off the root end and discard. Discard any damaged outer layers. Remove the feathery leaves. Slice each fennel bulb crosswise into thin slices. Place them in a bowl.
2. Section the oranges and place them in the bowl, adding to the bowl any extra orange juice.
3. Stir in the lemon juice and olive oil. Add salt and freshly ground black pepper. Toss. Cover and refrigerate for at least a half hour before serving.

Serves 4-6

Fennel and Celeriac Salad

A simple and refreshing side dish that is meant to be served cold.

1 large or 2 small fennel bulbs
1 celeriac (about 1¾ lbs or 800 g)
5 garlic cloves, chopped
3 tablespoons peanut oil
juice of 2 lemons
2 teaspoons sugar (or less)
salt and pepper to taste
2 tablespoons chopped flat-leafed parsley

1. Cut fennel bulbs in half, then cut halves into thick slices.
2. Peel the celeriac and cut into ¾-inch (2 cm) cubes. Keep in acidulated water to prevent it turning brown.
3. Fry the garlic in the oil until lightly colored. Add the fennel and celeriac and just enough water to cover the vegetables.
4. Add lemon juice, sugar and salt and pepper. Simmer covered, stirring occasionally, for 30 minutes. Remove lid and reduce liquid to a thick sauce.
5. Serve cold with the chopped parsley mixed in.

Serves 6

Fennel au Gratin

You don't have to be a cheese lover to appreciate how successfully fennel can be combined with cheese to make a very tasty dish.

2 fennel bulbs
1 oz (25 g) butter
1 oz (25 g) flour
5 fl oz (150 ml) milk
1 teaspoon mustard
3 oz (75 g) Cheddar cheese, grated
1 tablespoons breadcrumbs, crumbed

1. Cut the fennel into slices and cook them in boiling salted water for 5 minutes. Drain, setting aside 5 oz (150 ml) of the cooking water.
2. In a small pan melt the butter and stir in the flour. Gradually add the milk, stirring constantly. Pour in the reserved cooking water. Simmer for 2 minutes. Stir in the mustard and all but 2 tablespoons of the cheese.
3. Place fennel in an ovenproof dish and pour the sauce over the fennel.
4. Sprinkle remaining cheese and the breadcrumbs over the top. Place under a hot grill until browned and serve.

Serves 4

Italian Fennel Casserole

Prepared with tomatoes and garlic, this makes an excellent casserole.

3 fennel bulbs (1 lb or 450 g)
2 tablespoons olive oil
1 large onion, finely chopped
3 cloves garlic, crushed
14 oz (400 g) tin of tomatoes
salt and pepper
2 oz (50 g) fresh brown breadcrumbs
2 oz (50 g) grated Parmesan or Cheddar cheese

1. Slice fennel bulbs very thinly. Reserve some of the feathery tops for garnish.
2. Heat oil in a large pan and fry the chopped onion and garlic gently. Add the fennel slices and cook for a few minutes, turning them over in the pan.
3. Empty tin of tomatoes into a small bowl and crush them slightly with a spoon. Add the tomatoes to the fennel mixture and season with salt and freshly ground pepper. Cover pan and simmer for about 10 minutes, then transfer contents of pan to a lightly greased ovenproof casserole.
4. Mix cheese and breadcrumbs together and sprinkle the mixture over the top. Bake the casserole for about 20 minutes until top is browned and crisp.
5. Garnish with feathery fennel tops (optional) and serve.

Serves 4-6

Baked Fennel

Here's an Italian way of preparing fennel that brings out the delicate anise flavor.

3 large fennel bulbs
4 tablespoons olive oil
3 cloves garlic, minced
4 tablespoons chopped flat-leaf parsley
salt and pepper to taste
4 tablespoons breadcrumbs

1. Cut fennel heads lengthwise into 4 parts. Boil the fennel for about 15 minutes, until tender but still firm. Drain and arrange in a baking dish.
2. Mix the oil with the garlic, parsley and salt and freshly ground pepper. Pour the mixture over the fennel and turn them so that they are coated all over with the dressing.
3. Sprinkle with breadcrumbs. Bake in a hot oven at 400°F (200°C) for 15-20 minutes, or until golden in color.

Serves 4-6

Ragout of Fennel and Green Beans

Accompany this fragrantly-seasoned vegetable stew with crusty bread or a garlic baguette.

1 large fennel bulb (or 2 small ones)
1 lb (450 g) green beans
3 garlic cloves, minced
1 large onion, chopped
3 tablespoons olive oil
3 large potatoes, cut into ½ inch (1.2 cm) cubes
3 fresh tomatoes, chopped
1 teaspoon dried thyme
8 fl oz (225 ml or 1 cup) water
pinch of saffron
1½ teaspoons freshly grated orange peel
juice of half a lemon
salt and pepper to taste

1. Cut the fennel bulb into ¼-inch (.6 cm) slices. Cut the green beans into 1-inch (2.5 cm) pieces.
2. Sauté garlic and onions in the oil, stirring occasionally until onions are soft. Add potatoes and tomatoes. Sir in thyme and water. Cover and bring to a boil, then reduce heat to simmer.
3. Add green beans and fennel bulb. Mix in the saffron, orange peel, and lemon juice and allow to simmer for 15-20 minutes, stirring occasionally, until potatoes and green beans are tender. Add salt and freshly ground black pepper.

Serves 6

Green Beans

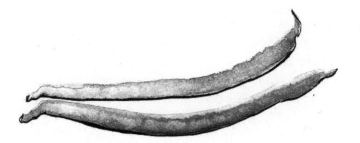

GREEN BEANS

Green beans, French beans, runner beans, haricots verts, yellow wax beans (obviously not green at all), broad beans, lima beams—all belong to a large family of legumes.

Beans are native to South America, and archeological evidence reveals that broad beans have been cultivated there since Neolithic times. They were a staple food in the Middle Ages and a source of protein for the poor. High in carbohydrates, they are also a source of vitamins A, B1 and B2, as well as potassium and iron.

Whether they're French beans or runner beans (which are favored in Britain), beans freeze well enough to keep you supplied all winter. Wash, trim, and cut the beans, pulling away any strings. Blanch for 2 minutes. Quickly place under cold running water to stop the cooking process and to retain the bright green color. Drain and pat dry. Place in freezer bags or containers. Or cook and serve cold, in an oil and vinegar dressing, as a salad.

After cooking, beans should have a crunchy texture. Otherwise, they are overcooked. One of the world's staple foods, beans are nutritious and easy to grow.

Broad beans are a particularly delicious vegetable when garden fresh. Just cook them until tender and serve with butter for a flavor revelation. Very young and small beans, no more than 3 inches (7.5 cm) in length, have tender pods and can be eaten whole. Older ones need to be shelled. Lima beans too may be cooked in a little boiling water until tender.

RECIPES for GREEN BEANS

APPETIZERS
French Bean Paté 96

SOUPS
Broad Bean Soup 97
Green Bean Soup 98
Cream of Fresh Bean Soup 100

SALADS
Green Bean Salad 101
Swiss Green Bean Salad 102
French Bean Salad with Mint 104
Dill Bean Salad 105

ACCOMPANIMENTS
Green Beans with Anchovies 106
Green Beans with Tomatoes 107
Green Beans with Cashews 108
Green Beans with Garlic and Pimento 109
Green Beans with Mushrooms 110
Green Beans with Water Chestnuts 111
Herbed Green Beans 112
Oriental Green Beans with Peanut Sauce 113
Stir-Fried Green Beans with Pine Nuts 114
Tuscany Style Green Beans 115
Runner Beans in Sour Cream 116
Spicy Indian Green Beans 117
Green Bean and Potato Curry 118

French Bean Paté

This makes a good spread for crackers or pitta bread and is easy to prepare with a food processor.

8 oz (225 g) French beans
1 onion, finely chopped
1 tablespoon olive oil
2 eggs, hard boiled
4 oz (100 g) walnuts
4 tablespoons dry white wine
2 tablespoons mayonnaise
juice of 1 lime
salt and pepper to taste

1. Cook the beans until tender.
2. Sauté the onion in oil until soft and transparent.
3. Place all the ingredients in a food processor and blend until smooth. Check seasonings.
4. Refrigerate in a covered bowl for at least two hours, until ready to use.

Broad Bean Soup

In season from April to September, young broad beans, which are soft and tender, can be cooked complete with pods to make a good summer soup.

2 lbs (1 kg) young broad bean pods
1 small onion, cut up
a handful of lettuce leaves
about 40 oz (1 litre) chicken stock
salt and pepper
sugar (optional)
about 10 fl oz (300 ml) milk
3 tablespoons cream
a few small cooked broad beans to garnish (optional)

!. Cut off ends of broad bean pods and place the pods in a saucepan with onion and torn-up lettuce leaves.
2. Pour in just enough chicken stock to cover and season with salt and pepper. Add some sugar if you want to.
3. Bring to a boil. Turn down heat and simmer, covered, until pods are soft. Strain off and reserve liquid.
4. Purée pod mixture in blender or food processor.
5. Boil cooking liquid to reduce it by half and add to purée. Add milk and reheat.
6. Correct seasonings and stir in the cream. Add a few shelled broad beans as a garnish just before serving.

Serves 6-8

Green Bean Soup

In addition to green beans, this soup uses nutritious broad beans and canned flageolet beans, each with a separate flavor—all blending to produce a pale green soup with a delicacy of its own.

8 oz (225 g) green beans
12 oz (350 g) broad beans
2 tablespoons olive oil
1 medium onion, chopped
1 clove garlic, crushed
35 fl oz (1 litre) chicken or vegetable stock
15 oz (425 g) can flageolet beans
salt and freshly ground black pepper to taste
chives to garnish (optional)

1. Wash green beans and top and tail them. Cut into 1-inch (2.5 cm) pieces. Remove broad beans from pods.
2. Heat the olive oil in a large saucepan and add the chopped onion and crushed garlic. Stir.
3. Add the green beans to the saucepan together with the broad beans. Cook for a few minutes.
4. Pour stock into the saucepan and boil for 5 minutes, then lower heat and cook for about 10 minutes. Remove saucepan from heat and stir in the can of flageolet beans with their liquid. Mix well.

5. Place the soup in a food processor and blend it into a purée. Return the purée to the saucepan. Season with salt and pepper and reheat when ready to use.
6. Garnish with chopped chives (if you want to) and serve.

Serves 4-6

Cream of Fresh Green Bean Soup

This soup, which may be served hot or cold, calls for very fresh green beans, ideally straight from the garden. It is so simple that the beans must be fresh and delicious all by themselves.

1½ lbs (700 g) fresh green beans,
16 fl oz (450 ml or 2 cups) milk, hot but not scalded
salt and pepper

1. Cut away tops and tails and remove strings from the beans. Steam them until just tender. Rinse in a colander with cold water to stop the cooking and retain the bright green color.
2. Using a food processor or blender, process the beans with the hot milk until you have a very smooth purée.
3. Season with salt and freshly ground pepper to taste.
4. Heat just before serving, being careful not to boil it. Or serve it cold.

Serves 4

Green Bean Salad

This salad is easy to prepare and makes a pleasant change from conventional green salads.

1 lb (450 g) French-style green beans
French dressing
chopped parsley (optional)
spring onions (optional)

1. Cook green beans in boiling water for about 5 minutes or until they are just tender and still crisp. Drain.
2. While they are still warm, dress with oil, vinegar, salt and freshly ground black pepper. Or use a good-quality prepared French dressing.
3. Add chopped parsley and chopped spring onions, if you want to.
4. Chill and allow to marinate for 24 hours before serving.

Serves 4

Swiss Green Bean Salad

Prepare this attractive-looking salad a day in advance and marinate overnight for most delicious results.

1½ lbs (700 g) green beans

Dressing Ingredients:
5 tablespoons lemon juice
2 large cloves garlic, crushed
4 fl oz (125 ml) olive oil
1 tablespoon red wine vinegar
½ teaspoon crushed tarragon
½ teaspoon dried dill weed
½ teaspoon salt
freshly ground black pepper
2 teaspoons Dijon mustard
4 tablespoons fresh parsley, chopped

5 oz (150 g) Swiss cheese, cut into thin strips
4 oz (100 g or ½ cup) ripe olives, chopped
half a green pepper, thinly sliced
half a red pepper, thinly sliced
4 oz (100 g or ½ cup) almonds, toasted and chopped

1. Steam the beans until just tender. Quickly rinse in cold water.
2. Combine the dressing ingredients in a large bowl and mix thoroughly.

3. Add the drained beans to the dressing. Add the strips of Swiss cheese and toss well. Cover and marinate for 2-3 hours, stirring from time to time.
4. Mix in the chopped olives and sliced peppers. Cover and chill overnight (or at least 5 hours).
5. Top with chopped toasted almonds before serving

4-6 servings

French Bean Salad with Mint

Use fresh and young beans, without strings. The mint, along with the other ingredients, produces a most wonderful flavor.

1 lb (450 g) French beans
1-2 garlic cloves
3-4 sprigs fresh mint
4 tablespoons olive oil
juice of 1 lemon
salt and pepper

1. Cook the beans until they are tender. Drain and place in a serving bowl.
2. Chop the garlic and the mint finely.
3. Mix the garlic and mint with the oil and lemon. Add salt and pepper to taste. Combine the mixture with the beans.
4. Mix well and serve hot or cold.

Serves 4-6

Dill Bean Salad

These intensely flavored beans make a great salad and will keep in the refrigerator for four days. Alternatively, serve hot for a terrific side dish.

1 lb (450 g) green beans
2 tablespoons fresh dill, chopped
2 large garlic cloves, crushed
¼ teaspoon red pepper flakes
3 fl oz (75 ml or 1/3 cup) cider vinegar
½ teaspoon honey or sugar
1 teaspoon vegetable oil

1. Cook the beans in boiling water for about 5 minutes, until bright green and just tender. Drain and place them in a bowl. Stir in the dill while the beans are still warm.
2. Combine in a saucepan the garlic, red pepper flakes, vinegar, and honey or sugar and bring to a boil. Simmer for 2 minutes.
3. Pour the dressing over the green beans. Add the oil and mix well.
4. Serve immediately. Or chill in refrigerator and serve cold.

Serves 4-6

Green Beans with Anchovies

If you like anchovies, you'll love green beans prepared with them.

1 lb (450 g) green beans
2 tablespoons oil
1 clove garlic, crushed
1½ oz (40 g) anchovies, finely minced

1. Boil the beans until tender but still crisp (about 5 minutes). Drain and pour cold water over them to stop them cooking.
2. Sauté garlic in the oil for a few minutes. Add the anchovies and stir briefly.
3. Add the beans. Cover and cook for about 3-5 minutes, until the beans are heated through.

Serves 4

Green Beans with Tomatoes

Use thin and tender green beans for this dish, which can be enjoyed hot or at room temperature.

4-5 tablespoons olive oil
1½ lbs (750 g) green beans
3 garlic cloves, finely chopped
1 medium onion, coarsely chopped
4 small tomatoes, peeled and roughly chopped
3-4 tablespoons chopped Italian parsley
4 tablespoons red wine vinegar
1½ teaspoons dried oregano
½ teaspoon salt
½ teaspoon freshly ground black pepper

1. Heat olive oil in a skillet and add beans. Cook and stir until beans are about half-cooked and become bright green.
2. Reduce heat. Add garlic and onions and continue to cook, stirring occasionally, for another minute.
3. Add tomatoes, parsley, vinegar, oregano, salt and pepper. Continue cooking, with occasional stirring, for about 5 minutes, or until sauce is slightly reduced. Serve hot or at room temperature.

Serves 4-6

Green Beans with Cashews

This recipe elevates the humble bean to an elegant status.

1½ lbs (750 g) green beans
3 tablespoons butter
½ teaspoon salt
½ teaspoon freshly ground black pepper
3-4 tablespoons chopped parsley
8 oz (225 g or 1 cup) cashews, coarsely chopped

1. Blanch the green beans in boiling salted water.
2. Melt the butter and stir in the salt and pepper and the parsley.
3. Drain the beans and place them in a warm serving bowl. Sprinkle cashews over the beans, then pour the butter mixture over the top.
4. Toss well and serve immediately.

Serves 6

Green Beans with Garlic and Pimento

Add color to your dinner with this interesting variation on simple boiled green beans.

1 lb (500 g) green beans
2 tablespoons oil
2 cloves garlic, crushed
½ teaspoon salt
3-4 tablespoons chopped pimento

1. Boil beans, uncovered, for about 5-7 minutes, or until tender but still crisp. Drain in a colander and pour cold water over them to stop the cooking. (This step can be done in advance.)
2. Heat the oil in a frying pan on medium heat and sauté the garlic.
3. Stir in the green beans, salt and pimento. Cover and cook only until the beans are heated through, about 3-5 minutes. Serve.

Serves 4-6

Green Beans with Mushrooms

Another easy variation on a green bean theme.

1 lb (450 g) green beans
2 tablespoons oil
½ lb (225 g) mushrooms, sliced
½ teaspoon salt

1. Boil beans for about 5-7 minutes, until tender but still crisp. Drain and pour cold water over them to stop the cooking process. (This step may be done in advance if you want to.)
2. Warm the oil in a frying pan over medium heat. Add mushrooms and cook, stirring until the mushrooms are almost done, about 5 minutes.
3. Stir in the green beans and salt. Cover and cook only until the beans are heated through, about 3-5 minutes. Serve.

Serves 4-6

Green Beans with Water Chestnuts

A simple way to add to your green bean repertory.

1 lb (450 g) green beans
8 oz (225 g) tin water chestnuts, drained and coarsely
  chopped
3 tablespoons butter
salt
pinch of oregano

1. Cook green beans in boiling water until tender. Drain.
2. Sauté drained and chopped water chestnuts in butter for about 3 minutes. Pour over hot beans. Season with salt and oregano and serve.

Serves 4

Herbed Green Beans

A savory way of adding flavor to your meal.

1 lb (500 g) green beans
3 tablespoons oil
1 small-medium onion, chopped
1 clove garlic, minced
half a stalk celery, chopped
½ teaspoon oregano
¼ teaspoon rosemary
½ teaspoon salt

1. Cut the beans into 2½ inch (6.3 cm) pieces.
2. Sauté the onion, garlic and celery in the oil for about 10 minutes.
3. Stir in the beans, herbs and salt. Cover and cook over low heat, stirring occasionally, until the beans are tender, about 12 minutes.

Serves 4

Oriental Green Beans with Peanut Sauce

Here is a recipe designed to turn ordinary beans into an extraordinary dish.

1 lb (450 g) French beans
2 tablespoons peanut butter
1 tablespoon soy sauce
1 tablespoon lemon juice
1 tablespoon water
2 teaspoons honey
1 clove garlic, minced
¼ teaspoon ground ginger

1. Cook French-style green beans until tender, about 5 minutes.
2. Combine remaining ingredients in a bowl and whisk until well blended.
3. When beans are cooked, drain them and place in a serving bowl. Spoon the peanut sauce mixture over the beans and serve.

Serves 4

Stir-Fried Green Beans with Pine Nuts

The stir-frying method leaves green beans crunchy, and the pine nuts add a bit more crunch.

2 tablespoons oil
1 lb (450 g) green beans, cut into 1-inch (2.5 cm) pieces
3 cloves garlic, finely chopped
1 medium onion, chopped
1 oz (25 g) pine nuts
1 tablespoon soy sauce
freshly ground black pepper
2 fl oz (50 ml or ¼ cup) water

1. Heat oil in a frying pan or wok over medium-high heat. Add green beans, garlic, onions, and pine nuts. Cook, stirring constantly, for 5-7 minutes, or until onions start to brown.
2. Stir in soy sauce, pepper to taste, and water. Reduce heat to medium-low. Cover and cook for about 5 minutes.

Serves 4

Tuscany Style Green Beans

This Italian method, which can also use French beans, produces a spicy dish that goes well with grilled meat or roasted poultry.

1 lb (450 g) runner beans
2 oz (50 g) butter
1 tablespoon olive oil
1 tablespoon chopped fresh sage or fresh parsley
1 large clove garlic, crushed
salt and freshly ground pepper to taste
1 tablespoon grated Parmesan cheese

1. Wash runner beans, cut off tops and tails and remove strings. Cut beans into 2-inch (5 cm) pieces. Cook in boiling water until just tender. Drain and cover with a cloth to keep warm.
2. Heat the butter and oil in a frying pan over moderate heat. Stir in half the sage or parsley and the crushed garlic. Fry for 1 minute. Add the beans. Season with salt and pepper. Stir over low heat for 5 minutes.
3. Mix in the Parmesan cheese. Sprinkle with remaining herbs and serve immediately.

Serves 4

Runner Beans in Sour Cream

When fresh runner beans first appear towards the end of July, try preparing them with this unusual dressing. (You can also use green beans.)

1 lb (450 g) runner beans
5 fl oz (150 ml) sour cream
grated nutmeg, to taste
salt and freshly ground black pepper
½ teaspoon caraway or dill seeds (optional)
2 oz (50 g) butter
1½ oz (40 g) course, white breadcrumbs

1. Top and tail the runner beans and slice them crossways into 1-inch (2.5 cm) segments. Cook in boiling water for 5 minutes. Drain.
2. Measure the sour cream into a bowl and season with nutmeg and salt and pepper, to taste. Add caraway or dill seeds if you want to. Toss beans in this dressing, coating them thoroughly.
3. Grease an ovenproof dish with some of the butter. Melt the remaining butter and mix in the breadcrumbs. Place beans in the dish and cover with breadcrumb mixture.
4. Bake in a preheated oven at 350°F (180°C) for about 15-20 minutes, until topping has browned.

Serves 4-6

Spicy Indian Green Beans

This Gujerati-style vegetable dish goes well with simple grilled or roasted meat or chicken. If you would like the beans to be quite hot, you can retain the chilli seeds.

1 lb (450 g) French beans
4 tablespoons vegetable oil
1 tablespoon whole black mustard seeds
4 cloves garlic, very finely chopped
½-1 dried and hot red chilli, seeded and crushed
1 teaspoon salt
½ teaspoon sugar
freshly ground black pepper

1. Cut beans into 1-inch (2.5 cm) lengths. Blanch them in boiling water for 3-4 minutes or until just tender. Drain quickly in a colander and rinse under cold, running water to stop the cooking and preserve the bright color. Set aside.
2. Heat the oil in a large frying pan over medium heat. When hot, add the mustard seeds and, as soon as they begin to pop, add the garlic. Stir until garlic turns light brown. Add crushed red chilli and stir for a few seconds.
3. Mix in the green beans, salt and sugar. Stir and cook for 7-8 minutes on medium-low heat or until beans have absorbed the spice flavors.
4. Mix in the black pepper and serve.

Serves 4

`Green Bean and Potato Curry

Another recipe from India that offers a special bonus if you have new potatoes from your garden. Enjoy the aroma!

10 oz (275 g) fine beans
1 lb (450 g) small new potatoes
1 oz (25 g) butter
3 tablespoons sunflower or vegetable oil
2 small green chillies
½ teaspoon cumin seeds
½ teaspoon ground turmeric
¼ teaspoon garam masala
1 clove garlic, crushed
salt to taste

1. Top and tail the green beans and cut them into 1-inch (2.5 cm) lengths. Scrub the potatoes and cut them into thick slices.
2. Heat the butter and oil in a frying pan over high heat. When they begin to sizzle, stir in the whole green chillies, the cumin seeds, turmeric, garam masala, and garlic. Fry for 30 seconds.
3. Add potatoes to the pan. Season with salt and stir until potatoes are well coated with the butter and oil.
4. Stir in the beans. Cover pan and reduce heat to moderate. Cook for 15 minutes, stirring occasionally, until potatoes are tender.

Serves 4

Kale and Collards

KALE AND COLLARDS

A member of the brassica family, kale includes a variety of green leafed vegetables, the most common being the curly leafed variety. The leaves are heavily crimped with thick ribs. Mostly available in early spring, this is a strong-tasting vegetable with a robust flavor that makes it a good partner for hotly-spiced foods and a favorite in many Indian dishes. It's best to select kale when the leaves are a dark green color with thin stems.

Collards are another variety, popular in the southern United States, perhaps because they tolerate heat well. Nevertheless, they are most sweet when grown in cool-weather climates. Indeed, they can even be harvested in the snow. Collards are best in late autumn. They are a sturdy vegetable that keeps well.

Kale and collards, a good source of vitamin A, are interchangeable in recipes. The only snag in cooking these greens is to make sure you cook them long enough to soften the stems, which are otherwise tough and chewy.

To prepare, if the stems are thick, remove them by cutting them away from the leaves and simply cooking them a little longer than the leaves. Kale and collards may be steamed, boiled, or stir-fried, or used in soup. They are done when the stems can be easily pierced with a skewer or thin-bladed knife.

RECIPES for KALE AND COLLARDS

SOUP
White Bean Soup with Greens 122
Asian Kale Soup with Lime 123

SALAD
Greek Salad of Cooked Greens 124

ACCOMPANIMENTS
Boiled Kale or Collards 125
Garlic Kale or Collards 126
Brazilian-Style Kale or Collards 127
Gingered Kale or Collards 128

White Bean Soup with Greens

This makes a hearty and enjoyable soup.

½ lb (225 g) dried white beans, washed and sorted
1 teaspoon fresh thyme leaves or ½ teaspoon dried
1 bay leaf
1 onion
½ lb (225 g) kale, collard, or other dark greens
salt and pepper to taste
40 fl oz (1.2 litres or 5 cups) chicken or vegetable stock
8 oz (225 g) rice
1 teaspoon minced garlic

1. In a large pot, combine the beans, thyme, bay leaf and onion. Cover with water and bring to a boil. Reduce heat and simmer until beans are tender, about 1 hour. Add water as necessary using only enough to cover beans.
2. Wash the greens. Separate leaves from stems. Roll the leaves up and slice them across the roll, then chop. Cut the stems into short lengths less than 1 inch (2.5 cm).
3. Remove onion and bay leaf from the pot and discard.
4. Season beans well and add stock. Bring to a boil. Add the greens stems and cook for 2 minutes. Then add the leaves and rice and cook, stirring occasionally, until rice is tender, about 15 minutes. Add water if necessary.
5. Stir in the garlic and cook for another minute. Adjust seasonings and serve.

Serves 4-6

Asian Kale Soup with Lime

This is a deliciously spicy soup that is quick and easy to make.

about 1 lb (450 g) kale leaves, roughly chopped
2 tablespoons peanut oil
1 medium-large onion, minced
2 garlic cloves, minced
32 fl oz (950 ml or 4 cups) chicken, beef, or vegetable stock
1 tablespoon soy sauce
cilantro leaves, finely chopped for garnish
1 stemmed and minced jalapeno chile (optional)
1 lime, cut into eight segments

1. Strip kale leaves from the stalks and rinse thoroughly.
2. Place the oil in a large saucepan on medium-high heat. Add the onion and cook, stirring occasionally, for 5-8 minutes, until it begins to turn golden.
3. When onion begins to color, add the garlic and cook for 1 minute. Add the stock and bring to a boil. Then turn heat to low and add the soy sauce.
4. Add the kale to the simmering broth and cook until kale is tender, about 10 minutes. You may stop here and refrigerate for up to 2 days. Reheat before continuing.
5. Taste for seasoning, adding more soy sauce (or salt) if you want to. Serve hot, garnished with chopped cilantro. Pass minced jalepeno and lime at the table.

Serves 4

Greek Salad of Cooked Greens

Here is an appealing salad of dark greens that also offers a useful way of using up leftovers.

1-2 lbs (450-900 g) dark greens such as kale, collards, spinach
2-3 tablespoons olive oil
salt and freshly ground black pepper
2 lemons, cut into halves

1. Trim the greens of any stems thicker than ¼ inch (.6 cm) and discard them. Wash the greens well.
2. Boil water in a large pot. Add the greens and simmer until tender, up to 10 minutes or more for tougher greens, a minute or two for spinach. Cool by running under cold water. Drain.
3. Squeeze the greens dry and chop them. (You may stop at this point and keep them covered in a refrigerator for a day before proceeding.)
4. Sprinkle the greens with olive oil and salt and pepper. Serve with lemon halves.

Serves 4

Boiled Kale or Collards

This basic method of preparing kale or collards is an easy and successful way to cook this sturdy green vegetable.

1-1½ lbs (450-700 g) kale or collards (or other dark green)
butter, olive oil, or lemon juice

1. Bring a pot of salted water to a boil.
2. If stems are more than ⅛ inch (.3 cm) thick, cut them away from the leaves and cook them in the pot of water for 5 minutes before adding the leaves. Cook until stems are tender enough to be pierced easily, about 5 to 15 minutes, depending on thickness.
3. Drain. Mix in a little butter, or olive oil or lemon juice and serve.

Serves 4

Garlic Kale or Collards

The sliced garlic mellows as it cooks with the greens. The second addition of garlic adds a strong flavor.

1 lb (450 g) kale or collards with thin stems
2 fl oz (50 ml or ¼ cup) olive oil
5-6 cloves garlic, sliced
½ teaspoon crushed red pepper flakes
salt and freshly ground black pepper to taste
4 fl oz (100 ml or ½ cup) chicken or vegetable stock
1 teaspoon minced garlic (or more)

1. Coarsely chop stems and leaves of the kale or collards.
2. Place olive oil in a saucepan and add the sliced garlic, red pepper flakes, and salt and pepper. Cook for about 1 minute over medium-high heat.
3. Add the greens and the stock. Cover and continue cooking over medium-high heat for about 5 minutes, or until greens are wilted and just tender but firm.
4. Remove the lid and continue to cook, stirring, until the liquid has almost evaporated and the greens are tender. Taste for seasoning and add pepper or salt as needed.
5. Add minced garlic. Cook for another minute and serve.

Serves 4

Brazilian-Style Kale or Collards

Use small greens for this dish as it cooks quite quickly.

1½ lbs (700 g) kale or collards
1 tablespoon olive or peanut oil
2-3 cloves garlic, minced
salt and freshly ground black pepper
juice of 1 small lemon

1. Chop the greens into small pieces.
2. Place oil in a frying pan over high heat until smoking.
3. Add the greens and the garlic and cook over high heat, stirring just until greens wilt and start to brown, about 3-6 minutes.
4. Season with salt and pepper. Add lemon juice and serve.

Serves 4

Gingered Kale or Collards

The ginger makes this a dish reminiscent of Chinese cooking.

1½ lbs (700 g) greens
2 tablespoons peanut oil
1-2 cloves garlic, minced
salt and freshly ground pepper to taste
1 tablespoon fresh grated or minced ginger
juice of 1 lime
chopped parsley for garnish

1. Shred the kale or collards.
2. Place oil in a large frying pan over medium-high heat. When hot, add greens and cook, stirring occasionally, for about 5-10 minutes.
3. When the greens are tender, add the garlic, salt and pepper. Continue to cook and stir for another 2 minutes.
4. Add the ginger and cook for another minute. Sprinkle in the lime juice. Garnish and serve.

Serves 4

Kohlrabi

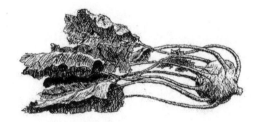

KOHLRABI

Kohlrabi is an odd-looking vegetable that somewhat resembles a spacecraft. It has long been familiar in oriental cooking but has recently become a fashionable vegetable in many cuisines.

A member of the brassica family, kohlrabi has a bulbous stalk that is edible rather than a flowering head. There are two varieties—purple and pale green, both with a mild flavor that some say is reminiscent of water chestnuts, others that it has a turnip-like taste. It is sometimes called a "cabbage-turnip" because it belongs to the cabbage family but is treated as if it were a turnip and is used in turnip recipes.

Kohlrabi is excellent raw or cooked. The bulbs, which should be young and small, not much larger than a golf ball, may be simply steamed or boiled. Larger bulbs can be hollowed out and stuffed, with fried onions and tomatoes for instance.

It can be eaten raw with a dip or in a grated salad like coleslaw. Or diced and added to a green salad. It can be cooked and diced and made into a salad like potato salad.

The greens, if fresh, are milder than turnip or collard greens and may also be eaten. Wash thoroughly, remove stems and heavy ribs, then blanch in boiling water until tender (8 to 10 minutes) and serve with butter. Or sauté greens briefly in oil and garlic.

It's worth experimenting with this exotic vegetable.

RECIPES for KOHLRABI

SALAD

ACCOMPANIMENTS

Kohlrabi and Apple Salad

This gets far away from customary salads.

1 kohlrabi bulb
1 apple
2½ fl oz (60 ml) heavy or double cream
1 tablespoon fresh lemon juice
1 tablespoon wholegrain mustard
¼ teaspoon sugar
salt and pepper to taste
sunflower seeds (optional)

1. Peel the kohlrabi and cut into strips. Core and dice the apple.
2. Whip the cream until it forms soft peaks. Add remaining ingredients and whisk together.
3. Mix in the kohlrabi and apple. Sprinkle with sunflower seeds if you want to and serve.

Serves 4

Boiled Kohlrabi

Once the kohlrabi is cooked, you can also serve it mashed or puréed. Or you can top with cheese and bake it au gratin.

1 lb kohlrabi (450 g)
salt and freshly ground black pepper
butter

1. To prepare, cut off the leaves around the bulb and trim off the tapering roots. Scrub the bulb in cold water and peel it. Small globes can be left whole. Larger ones may be sliced or diced.
2. Boil kohlrabi in a pot of salted water for about a half hour, depending on size. Drain when tender.
3. Sprinkle with salt and pepper and toss with melted butter, or serve with a white sauce.

Serves 4

Braised Kohlrabi

The choice of liquid used for braising will determine much of the flavor. Covering and slow cooking will help to preserve and intensify intrinsic flavors.

1 lb (450 g) kohlrabi
small onion, chopped
salt and pepper to taste
3-4 tablespoons white wine or stock

1. Prepare the kohlrabi by scrubbing and peeling. If the bulb is large, cut into slices.
2. Heat oil in a pan and add the kohlrabi and chopped onion. Sprinkle with salt and freshly ground black pepper and sauté until brown.
3. Add white wine or stock to the pan. Cover and simmer for up to 1 hour, or until tender (depending on size). Add more liquid if necessary.

Serves 4

Braised Kohlrabi with Garlic

Another method for braising. You might want to double quantities for more generous servings of this side dish.

1 kohlrabi bulb
1 teaspoon butter
1-2 cloves garlic, minced
7 fl oz (200 ml) chicken stock
salt and pepper to taste
freshly grated Parmesan cheese

1. Peel the kohlrabi and cut into strips.
2. Melt butter in frying pan over medium heat. Add the kohlrabi and garlic and sauté for 2-3 minutes
3. Add the stock and bring to the boil. Turn down heat and simmer, covered, for 15 minutes or until tender. Season with salt and pepper.
4. Sprinkle with Parmesan cheese and serve.

Serves 2-4

Kohlrabi Stuffed with Peppers

If you are not very familiar with kohlrabi, or have eaten it only in stews where its flavor is obscured, this is a good dish to try. The slight peppery tang makes a good balance to the more earthy kohlrabi.

4 small kohlrabi, about 6-8 oz (175-225g) each
14 fl oz (400 ml or 1⅔ cup) vegetable stock
1 tablespoon olive oil
1 onion, chopped
1 small red pepper, seeded and sliced
1 small green pepper, seeded and sliced
salt and pepper to taste
flat leaf parsley for garnish (optional)

1. Trim the kohlrabi, cutting off tops and tails, and arrange them in an ovenproof dish.
2. Pour the stock into the vegetables to halfway up. Cover and place in oven preheated to 350°F (180°C) until tender, about 30 minutes. Transfer to a plate and allow to cool. Reserve the stock.
3. Heat the oil in a frying pan and fry the onion gently for 3-4 minutes, stirring occasionally. Add the peppers and continue to cook a further 2-3 minutes, until onion is lightly browned.
4. Add the reserved vegetable stock and salt and pepper. Simmer, uncovered, until stock has almost evaporated.

5. Scoop the flesh from centers of kohlrabi leaving shells. Chop the flesh roughly and stir into the onion and pepper mixture. Adjust the seasonings.
6. Spoon this filling into the shells, and arrange shells in a shallow ovenproof dish. Place dish in oven for 5-10 minutes until heated through. Garnish with parsley if you want to and serve.

Serves 4

Sautéed Kohlrabi and Leeks

This harmonious combination of two green vegetables produces a lovely dish to accompany almost any main course.

8 kohlrabi, 1½ -2 inch (4-5 cm) diameter
3-4 medium leeks
4 tablespoons butter
salt and pepper to taste

1. Peel the kohlrabi and cut into thin slices. Trim roots and dark leaves from leeks, cut them lengthwise, wash thoroughly; and cut crosswise into thin slices.
2. Melt butter in a large frying pan. Add kohlrabi slices and sauté for 2 to 3 minutes. Add leeks and continue to sauté until kohlrabi has begun to soften and leeks are slightly browned. Season to taste and serve.

Serves 4-6

Miscellaneous Greens

MISCELLANEOUS GREENS

The list of greens is seemingly endless—in particular, Chinese greens. An amazingly large variety of greens on display in Chinese supermarkets include mustard greens, Chinese cabbage, Chinese broccoli, and pak choy.

Chinese mustard greens, which belong to the cabbage family, are grown in Europe for their mustard seeds and in India for their oil seeds. But the Chinese prefer the deep green, slightly crinkled leaves with their mustard flavor. Young leaves can be added to salads. Older leaves can be stir-fried with onion and garlic to make a great side dish.

Chinese cabbage, also called Napa cabbage, has pale green leaves with long, white ribs and a shape reminiscent of a fat head of celery. Crunchy, with a pleasant cabbage flavor, it can be stir-fried and is especially good with garlic or ginger.

Pak choy has thick stalks, vaguely recalling celery, with large spoon-shaped leaves. Its pleasant flavor has more bite than Chinese cabbage. Cut stalk and leaves into slices and stir-fry with garlic and onions.

Chinese broccoli looks somewhat like our own familiar broccoli but with slender heads of flowers, usually white or yellow. It can be cooked like Chinese mustard greens.

Beet greens are sometimes grown only for their greens, which make a tasty dish. Turnip tops, like beet greens, are delicious and nutritious. As they are not widely available, gardeners have a real advantage in being able to grow their own. Preparation is easy. Simply slice them and boil or steam for a few minutes. Serve with butter.

RECIPES for MISCELLANEOUS GREENS

ACCOMPANIMENTS

Beet Greens with Garlic

For this very simple but sprightly dish, you can also use Swiss chard, spinach, or other greens.

1 lb (450 g) beet greens
2-3 tablespoons butter
1 clove garlic, minced
salt and pepper to taste

1. Wash the leaves, trim the stems and break the leaves into pieces.
2. Warm the butter in a large pan over medium heat and cook the garlic for a minute or two.
3. Add the greens and seasonings. Cook and stir for about 3-5 minutes, just until the leaves wilt.

Serves 4

Stir-Fried Greens

Use a mixture of greens, or simply select one. Just be sure to add the slower-cooking vegetables earlier than the quicker-cooking ones. The stir-frying technique offers advantages: High temperature seals in juices to give crisp but tender vegetables. Quick cooking helps retain vitamins and minerals. It can be done in a relatively short time.

spinach
Swiss chard
kale
collards
pak choy
Chinese cabbage
peanut or vegetable oil
seasonings: tamari, crushed garlic, grated ginger, crushed hot pepper, sesame oil, wine
optional extas: chopped and toasted nuts, sliced water chestnuts, tofu, sesame seeds, mushrooms

1. Prepare the vegetables, cut them and place them in groups according to their respective cooking times.
2. Heat the oil in a large frying pan or wok. If you want to use onions, add them at this point and sauté them first.
3. Add greens and cook quickly over high heat, stirring almost constantly so that each vegetable is done to its own perfection.
4. Prepare in advance whichever seasonings and optional extras you want, and add them during last few minutes of cooking.

Spicy Greens

Fortunately, healthful greens are always available, and this dish can be made with mustard greens, kale, collard, beet greens, chard, spinach, pak choy . . . . You can also vary it by adding a small can of crushed tomatoes or cooked potato cubes, or a cup or two of peas or lima beans.

about 2 lbs (900 g) greens
1 large onion, diced
1 tablespoon olive oil
2 teaspoons vinegar
¼ teaspoon crushed red pepper flakes
salt and freshly ground black pepper

1. Wash the greens and coarsely chop, discarding any large stem ends.
2. Sauté the onion in the oil until soft. Add greens and cook with lid on for about 5 minutes or until greens are wilted but still bright green.
3. Stir in the vinegar and red pepper flakes. Add salt and pepper to taste and serve.

Serves 4-6

Pasta with Greens

You can use almost any green for this pleasing pasta dish.

1 bunch watercress (about 1 cup)
1 lb (450 g) Swiss chard
2 garlic cloves, minced
1 tablespoon olive oil
salt and pepper to taste
¼ teaspoon nutmeg
4 oz (100 g) ricotta cheese
1 lb (450 g) pasta (shells, penne, macaroni, fusilli, etc.)
grated Parmesan cheese
chopped fresh tomatoes
toasted pine nuts

1. Wash the watercress and chard and remove any tough stems. Chop coarsely.
2. Sauté the garlic in the oil until soft. Add the greens and sauté, stirring often, until they are wilted but still bright green. Sprinkle with salt, freshly ground fresh pepper, and nutmeg. Remove from heat.
3. Place the cooked greens and the ricotta in a blender or food processor and purée until smooth and evenly colored. Taste and add more salt and pepper if necessary.
4. Cook the pasta in boiling water until al dente. Drain and toss it immediately with the sauce in a warm serving bowl.
5. Top with Parmesan cheese, chopped tomatoes, and pine nuts and serve.

Serves 4-6

Gingered Greens and Tofu

*Highly nutritious greens, prepared with ginger and
cilantro, make this a terrific stir-fry.*

**about 1½ lbs (700 g) coarsely shredded greens (such as
Swiss chard, Chinese cabbage, or pak choy)
2 fl oz (50 ml) peanut oil
2 tablespoons grated fresh ginger
3 tablespoons lime juice
2 tablespoons fresh lime juice
2 tablespoons chopped fresh cilantro
pinch of cayenne
2 cakes (about 1½ lbs or 700 g) tofu**

**Marinade ingredients:
4 fl oz (100 ml or ½ cup) soy sauce
4 fl oz (100 ml or ½ cup) dry sherry
2 fl oz (50 ml or ¼ cup) rice vinegar
3 tablespoons brown sugar**

1. Prepare the greens. Measure the next 6 ingredients and
   have them ready before beginning to stir-fry.
2. Place marinade ingredients in a saucepan and bring to a
   boil. Simmer for 1 minute, then remove from heat.
3. Cut blocks of tofu into ½-inch (1.2 cm) slices, then cut
   slices into 1-inch (2.5 cm) squares and arrange them in a
   single layer in a heatproof pan. Pour the marinade over
   the squares. Sprinkle 2 tablespoons of the oil over the
   top and allow to stand for about 5 minutes. Grill or broil
   the tofu for 7-8 minutes, until lightly browned. Turn
   over and brown the other side.

4. Meanwhile, heat the remaining 2 tablespoons of oil in a large skillet or wok. Stir in the ginger and greens. Keep stirring on high heat until the greens wilt. When they are just tender, add lime juice, cilantro, and cayenne. Remove from heat.
5. When the tofu is browned, toss it gently with the marinade and cooked greens. Reheat if necessary. Serve immediately.

Serves 4-6

Turnip Tops with Garlic and Parmesan

As turnip tops have a strong flavor, it's best to cook them with other strongly-flavored ingredients such as garlic and Parmesan. Cooking does not take long as the leaves are tender.

12 oz (350 g) turnip tops
3 tablespoons olive oil
2 garlic cloves, crushed
4 spring onions, sliced
2 fl oz (50 ml or ¼ cup) water
salt and pepper to taste
2 oz (50 g) Parmesan cheese, grated
Parmesan cheese shavings to garnish (optional)

1. Slice the turnip tops thinly and remove tough stalks.
2. Heat the oil in a large pan and fry garlic very briefly. Add the spring onions and fry for 2 minutes. Add the turnip tops and stir-fry until the greens are coated in oil.
3. Add the water and bring to a boil. Cover and simmer, stirring occasionally, until the greens are tender.
4. Bring the water to a boil and cook until excess liquid evaporates. Add salt and pepper and stir in the grated Parmesan cheese. Sprinkle with cheese shavings if you want to and serve.

Serves 4

Peas

PEAS

Peas are a wonderful treat straight from the garden. Unfortunately the season is short, but fortunately you can eat like royalty for three or four weeks in early summer.

Peas are high in proteins and carbohydrates, but they seem to lose their flavor quickly once picked. If you are not going to use them right away, refrigerate them unshelled. Peas are best eaten raw out of the pod or cooked in a minimum of water, seasoned with salt and pepper and butter and served immediately. They are done as soon as they are hot and bright green, usually under five minutes.

Sugar snap peas, the sweetest of young peas, may be eaten pods and all. They can be served raw with a dip or sautéed in butter for 2 or 3 minutes or until heated through.

Snow peas (also called mange-tout or "eat all") have tiny peas or none inside the edible pods. These and sugar snaps need to be topped and tailed and strings removed. One quick preparation method is to stir-fry snow peas with sliced mushrooms (optional) in a little butter or oil. For an Oriental taste, add soy sauce instead of salt and a pinch of ground ginger.

Petits pois are a dwarf variety, not available fresh in shops as they are mainly grown commercially for canning or freezing. But gardeners grow their own.

RECIPES for PEAS

SOUPS

SALADS

ACCOMPANIMENTS

Cream of Curried Pea Soup

A cold curried soup for a warm spring or summer evening.

1 lb (450 g) shelled fresh peas
1 medium onion, sliced
1 small carrot, sliced
1 stalk celery with leaves, sliced
1 medium potato, sliced
1 clove garlic
1 teaspoon salt
1 teaspoon curry powder
16 fl oz (450 ml or 2 cups) chicken stock
8 fl oz (225 ml or 1 cup) cream

1. Place vegetables, seasonings and one cup stock in a saucepan and bring to a boil. Reduce heat and simmer covered for 15 minutes.
2. Transfer to a food processor or electric blender. Cover and process on high. Remove cover and, with motor running, pour in the remaining stock and cream.
3. Chill and serve.

Serves 6

Cream of Pea Soup with Tarragon

This light and simple-to-make soup is delicious hot or chilled.

1 bunch spring onions, finely chopped
3 oz (75 g) butter
1 lb (450 g) fresh peas, shelled
5 fl oz (150 ml) water
20 fl oz (575 ml) single or light cream
1-2 teaspoons fresh tarragon
salt and freshly ground black pepper

1. Clean the spring onions and chop finely, reserving some of the green pieces for garnish.
2. Melt the butter in a saucepan on low heat. Add the chopped spring onions, peas, and water. Cook until the peas are tender, about 20 minutes. Allow to cool slightly. Then stir in the cream and fresh tarragon. Season with salt and pepper to taste.
3. Place the soup into a food processor or electric blender and process until smooth. Spoon it into a clean pan. Re-heat gently when ready to serve. Garnish each bowl with the remaining chopped green spring onions.

Serves 6

Minted Peas and Spinach Soup

This elegant soup makes a great beginning to a special dinner.

4 tablespoons butter
2 medium onions, chopped
10 oz (275 g) spinach, chopped
24 fl oz (675-700 ml or 3 cups) chicken stock
10 oz (275 g) peas, shelled
small bunch fresh mint
8 fl oz (225 ml or 1 cup) heavy or double cream
salt and pepper to taste

1. In a large saucepan melt the butter and add the onions. Cover and cook over low heat until tender, about 20-25 minutes.
2. Wash and chop spinach and squeeze out excess water.
3. Pour stock into the saucepan. Add the spinach and the peas and bring to a boil. Then reduce heat and simmer, partially covered, until peas are tender, 15-20 minutes.
4. Rinse mint leaves and add them to the saucepan. Cover and simmer for another 5 minutes.
5. Strain the soup, reserving the liquid. Transfer the solids to a food processor together with about 8 oz (225 ml or 1 cup) of the cooking liquid. Process until smooth.
6. Transfer the puréed soup to the saucepan. Add the cream. Add about 8 oz (225 ml or 1 cup) of additional cooking liquid, until the soup is of the right consistency.
7. Add salt and pepper and simmer until heated through.

Serves 6

Garlic Soup with Peas

Simple garlic soups are found in peasant cooking all over the world. Peas are added to this basic garlic soup, a pleasant addition to country-style cuisine.

4 tablespoons olive oil
8 cloves garlic, peeled
1 tablespoon ground cumin
4 oz (100 g or ½ cup) orzo or long grain rice
32 fl oz (900 ml or 4 cups) chicken stock
salt and pepper
8 oz (225 g) peas, shelled
fresh minced parsley for garnish

1. Place oil in saucepan on medium heat. Add the garlic cloves and cook, stirring occasionally, until they are golden brown. Add the cumin and cook and stir for about a minute.
2. Remove the garlic cloves and set them aside. Reduce heat to medium-low and add the orzo or rice. Cook and stir to coat the orzo or rice with oil.
3. Pour in the stock and add salt and freshly ground black pepper to taste. Chop the garlic coarsely and return it to the pot. Add peas and cook, stirring occasionally, until the rice is tender, about 10 to 15 minutes.
4. Garnish with minced parsley and serve.

Serves 4-6

Rice and Pea Salad

Any rice will do, but Arborio rice is especially good. The salad may be prepared a day in advance and kept covered in the refrigerator. But remember to bring it to room temperature before serving.

8 oz (225 g or ½ cup) fresh peas, shelled
8 oz (225 g or 1 cup) Arborio rice
1-2 shallots, minced
juice of half a lemon
6-8 tablespoons olive oil
3-4 tablespoons fresh parsley leaves, minced
salt and pepper to taste

1. Place peas in a small pot of boiling salted water for about 2 minutes. Rinse in cold water to stop the cooking. Drain and set aside.
2. To a large pot of boiling salted water, add the rice. Cook and stir until the rice is tender, about 15 minutes. Drain and rinse quickly under cold water to stop the cooking.
3. Stir the shallots into the rice and mix well. Mix in the lemon juice and olive oil. Add parsley and salt and freshly ground pepper. Mix in the peas. Taste and adjust seasonings. Serve at room temperature.

Serves 4-6

Minted Peas and Radish Salad

Here's a spring salad with an attractive array of colors and tastes.

2 lbs (900 g) shelled peas
about 12 medium-size radishes, thinly sliced
3 tablespoons thinly sliced spring onions
1 stalk celery, chopped
1 teaspoon finely chopped fresh mint
1 tablespoon mayonnaise
2 tablespoons sour cream
freshly ground black pepper

1. Add peas to a saucepan of boiling salted water and cook them until they are barely tender, about 4-5 minutes. Rinse in cold water to stop the cooking. Drain well.
2. Mix together the peas, radishes, spring onions, celery, and mint. Chill for at least 1 hour.
3. Just before serving, stir in the mayonnaise, sour cream, and a dash of pepper.

Serves 4-6

Buttered Fresh Peas

Fresh peas are so delicious that you'll have to resist the temptation to eat them raw while shelling.

2 lbs (900 g) fresh peas, shelled
1-2 tablespoons butter
salt and pepper to taste
2 tablespoons fresh mint or basil, minced (optional)

1. Place peas in a small amount of boiling salted water. Cover and simmer until just tender, about 3 minutes, just until the peas are bright green and tender. Drain.
2. Melt butter in a frying pan over medium heat. When melted, turn heat to low and cook peas with salt and pepper and optional herb for 2-3 minutes, shaking pan occasionally (stirring with a utensil breaks the peas), just until peas are hot and coated with butter.

Serves 4-6

French Style Peas

Although slightly more complicated, this recipe is worth the effort.

2 lbs (900 g) shelled peas
6 tiny white onions, peeled
5 or 6 lettuce leaves, shredded
3 sprigs parsley
½ teaspoon salt
pinch of sugar
3 tablespoons butter
2 fl oz (50 ml or ¼ cup) water
1 teaspoon flour

1. Combine in a saucepan the peas, onions, lettuce, parsley, salt, sugar and 2 tablespoons of the butter. Mix together and add water.
2. Cook over medium heat with a tight-fitting lid until just a little moisture remains, about 30 minutes.
3. Cream together the remaining tablespoon of butter and the flour. Add to the pan and mix it by shaking the pan in a circular movement. (Don't break the peas by stirring with a utensil.)
4. When the liquid has thickened and returned to a boil, remove pan from heat. Remove parsley and serve.

Serves 4-6

Peas and Cocktail Onions

Some easy tricks can dress up a simple serving of peas. Instead of cocktail onions, you can substitute fresh baby onions, halved if necessary, or the white parts of spring onions. Just fry them in butter for 5-6 minutes before mixing them in with the peas.

2 lbs (900 g) fresh green peas
small jar of cocktail onions
butter
2 oz (50 ml or ¼ cup) sour cream (optional)

1. Cook peas in boiling salted water until they are tender. Drain them and mix together with the cocktail onions. Dress with butter and serve.
2. If you opt to add sour cream, return drained peas and onions to saucepan and mix in the sour cream. Heat through, being careful not to overcook.

Serves 4

Puréed Green Peas

Sweet tender peas are wonderful eaten raw straight from the pod. But as you do the relaxing work of shelling peas, try to save enough for this recipe.

2 lbs (900 g) fresh peas, shelled
¼ teaspoon sugar
3 tablespoons butter
2 tablespoons flour
4 fl oz (100 ml or ½ cup) cream
salt and pepper to taste
2 oz (50 ml or ¼ cup) sour cream

1. Place peas in a minimum amount of boiling salted water. Then reduce heat and simmer covered for about 4 minutes or until barely tender. Drain. Purée in a food processor or electric blender.
2. Melt the butter in a saucepan. Add flour and cook and stir until lightly browned. Add the pea purée and the cream and bring to a boil stirring constantly.
3. Season with salt and freshly ground black pepper and stir in the sour cream. Serve.

Serves 6-8

Italian Peas or Piselli

Another delicious and deliciously easy recipe for peas.

3 tablespoons vegetable oil
1 medium onion, finely chopped
2 lettuce leaves, cut into thin strips
1 lb (500 g) shelled peas
4 fl oz (125 ml) dry white wine
salt and freshly ground pepper to taste
½ teaspoon sugar (optional)

1. Place oil in pan and fry onions until they are translucent. Stir in the lettuce and peas.
2. Add the wine, salt and pepper, and sugar and simmer until peas are tender, about 5 to 10 minutes.

Serves 4

Indian Peas and Potatoes

A classic Indian dish with a delicious blend of vegetables and spices.

2 tablespoons vegetable oil
1 medium-large onion, chopped
2 cloves garlic, chopped
1 tin (1 lb or 450 g) tomatoes, chopped, undrained
2 medium potatoes, cut into ½-inch (1.2 cm) cubes
1 teaspoon curry powder
¼ teaspoon chili powder
½ teaspoon turmeric
1 bay leaf
8 fl oz (225 ml or 1 cup) water
1 lb (450 g) peas

1. Heat oil in a large frying pan over medium heat. Cook onions and garlic until soft, about 10 minutes.
2. Add remaining ingredients, except peas. Mix well and bring to a boil, stirring frequently. Reduce heat to low, and simmer covered for 15 minutes.
3. Mix in the peas. Cover and cook for another 20 minutes, or until potatoes are tender. Discard bay leaf and serve.

Serves 8

Stir-Fried Snow Peas or Sugar Snap Peas

Preparation of this delectable dish requires so little effort.

2 tablespoons peanut or other oil
1½ lbs (700 g) snow or sugar snap peas, washed and
   trimmed
2 tablespoons soy sauce
1 teaspoon sesame oil (optional)

1. Place oil in a large frying pan or wok on high heat. When the oil begins to smoke, add the peas and cook, stirring almost constantly for about 5 minutes or until they are bright green and glossy.
2. Remove from heat and spoon peas into a serving dish. Sprinkle soy sauce over the peas—and sesame oil, if you want to. Serve.

Serves 4

Peppers

PEPPERS

Peppers and chillies are members of the capsicum family. But to distinguish between them, peppers are called sweet peppers or bell peppers or capsicums. They come in a variety of colors—green, red, yellow, white, orange, and purple-black. In addition to the usual bell-shaped peppers, there are longer, slimmer shapes and miniatures.

Green peppers are mature but not ripe. Picked a week or two later, the same pepper will be red, yellow, or orange and have a sweet and more mellow flavor.

Green peppers are delicious raw in salads or cooked in many, many dishes. They make excellent containers for stuffings and are attractive when filled with colorful vegetables.

Peppers need to be cored and stemmed, unless you are roasting them whole. To prepare for stuffing, cut off the top, then cut away the inner core and pith and shake out the seeds. Best cooking methods include roasting, grilling, broiling, sautéing.

To roast, cut them into large pieces, place in a roasting pan, and sprinkle with olive oil, basil and seasoning. Roast in a very hot oven for about a half hour, turning occasionally.

Among the countless ways of cooking peppers is the popular ratatouille (from Provence). Slice them and fry in olive oil with onions and garlic. Aubergines (eggplant) can also be added. Then braise with tomatoes and herbs until vegetables are tender.

RECIPES for PEPPERS

STARTERS AND SALADS

SOUPS

ACCOMPANIMENTS

LUNCH OR SUPPER COURSE

Pepper and Tomato Chutney

Autumn, when there is an abundant harvest, is a good time for indulging in this easy and pleasant type of cookery. Using fresh vegetables and good quality spices and vinegar, you can produce a curry worthy to be part of the Indian legacy.

5 large peppers (any color)
3 lbs (1.4 kg) tomatoes
1 lb (450 g) apples
3 large onions
2 tablespoons salt
1½ lbs (700 g) sugar
40 fl oz (1.2 litres) white vinegar
2 oz (50 g) pickling spice

1. Seed the peppers and remove all white pith. Scald the tomatoes and skin them. Peel and core the apples. Peel the onions. Chop them all finely, or put them through a mincer.
2. Place all ingredients in a large pot. Add the salt, sugar, and vinegar.
3. Add the pickling spice. (Alternatively, you can make your own spice mixture using peppercorns, allspice berries, chillies, ginger, cloves, and mustard seed to taste.) Tie the spices up in a muslin bag.
4. Simmer for about 2 hours until the chutney is thick. Remove the bag of spices.
5. Pour into hot jars. Cover and seal.

Pickled Peppers

These peppers will keep for months if they are well covered with oil.

green or red peppers or a mixture of both
olive oil
wine vinegar
chopped garlic clove (optional)

1. Roast the peppers by placing them under a grill and turning them until the skins are black and blistered. Or roast them in a very hot oven for a half hour, turning them once, until skin is black. When cool, peel off the skins.
2. Remove the stems and the seeds and fibers. Cut the peppers into strips and put them into a jar.
3. Combine equal amounts of oil and vinegar and pour the mixture over the peppers. Make sure there is enough liquid to cover the peppers. Add garlic if you want to. Cover the jar and refrigerate.
4. Before serving, drain peppers and place them in a serving dish.

Stuffed Peppers with Rice

Peppers make good containers for an endless number of stuffings. This cold vegetarian recipe makes a good first course or a light meal and is useful for serving at buffet parties. Choose peppers that can stand on their base. Italian risotto rice, which sticks together, is another good choice.

6 green peppers
1 large onion, finely chopped
6 tablespoons olive oil
9 oz (250 g) rice
16 fl oz (450 ml or 2 cups) water
salt and pepper
1 teaspoon sugar
3 tablespoons pine nuts
3 tablespoons raisins
1 large tomato, peeled and chopped
2 teaspoons dried mint
3 tablespoons chopped flat-leafed parsley
juice of 1 lemon

1. To make the stuffing, fry the onion in 3 tablespoons oil until soft. Add rice and stir until well coated. Pour in the water and add salt and pepper and sugar. Mix well. Cover and cook for 15 minutes or until water has been absorbed but rice is not quite done. Mix in the remaining oil and the rest of the ingredients.

2. To stuff the peppers, cut a circle around the stem ends and keep the cut off circle with its stem to use as a top. Remove the core and seeds and spoon in the rice mixture. Cap each pepper with the stem-top.
3. Arrange the peppers alongside each other in a shallow baking dish. Pour in about an inch (2.5 cm) of water at the bottom. Bake in oven preheated to 375°F (190°C) for 45-50 minutes, or until peppers are tender. Remove from oven sooner if peppers look as if they may break.

Serves 6

Italian Pepper Salad

Once they are grilled and skinned, peppers reveal a soft and luxurious texture and are superb in salads. This excellent pepper salad goes well with grilled steaks or chops or roast chicken.

2 large green peppers
4 tablespoons olive oil
1 tablespoon wine vinegar or lemon juice
salt and freshly ground black pepper to taste

1. Char the peppers by securing them on a fork or skewer and holding them over a high flame of a gas burner. Turn until they are black all over. (Alternatively, they may be placed under the grill or roasted in a hot oven.) Peel off the outer charred skin.
2. Cut the peppers in half and remove the stem and seeds. Slice peppers into thin strips.
3. Place strips in a serving bowl and mix in the oil, vinegar, salt and pepper. Allow to stand a half hour at room temperature minutes before serving.

Serves 4

Spanish Pisto

*This typical Spanish dish makes a delightful first course.
Topped with poached or fried eggs, or with eggs scrambled
into it, it can also be the main dish of a light meal.*

4 tablespoons olive oil
1 large onion, finely chopped
2 cloves garlic, crushed
1 teaspoon chopped parsley
3 green (or red) peppers, seeded and sliced
1 lb (450 g) tomatoes, skinned, seeded, chopped
1 lb (450 g) courgettes, peeled and chopped
½ lb (225 g) new potatoes
salt and pepper

1. Heat the oil in a large frying pan and add the onions and
   garlic and the parsley. Cook slowly with the lid on until
   soft.
2. Add the peppers and continue to cook over low heat,
   covered, for another 10 minutes.
3. Add the tomatoes and courgettes. Cover and cook slowly
   for a half hour. Ten minutes before the end of cooking,
   stir in the diced potatoes, which have been separately
   fried in olive oil until golden in color and tender.
4. Season well and serve.

Serves 6-8

Moroccan Green Pepper Salad

Green peppers with tomatoes and lemon—a delight for the palate.

3 green peppers
3 ripe tomatoes, seeded and diced
rind of half a lemon, finely diced
1 tablespoon lemon juice
3 tablespoons chopped flatleaf parsley
1½ tablespoons olive oil
salt and freshly ground fresh pepper

1. Grill the peppers, turning them until the skin is black and blistered. When cool, peel off the skin and cut into salad size pieces Discard seeds and stems.
2. Place the peppers in a serving bowl with all the other ingredients and mix together.
3. Taste and adjust the seasoning. When ready to serve, either cold or at room temperature, drain off any excess liquid.

Serves 4

Basque Pepper and Rice Soup

Here's a comforting soup that tastes even better if made the day before you serve it.

6 tablespoons olive oil
3 small-medium onions, chopped
2 carrots, chopped
6 garlic cloves, chopped
56 fl oz (1.7 litres or 7 cups) beef stock
4 fl oz (100 ml or ½ cup) medium-dry sherry
2 green and 2 red bell peppers, cut into strips
4 oz (100 g or ½ cup) rice
salt and pepper to taste

1. In a large saucepan, heat the olive oil and add the onions, carrots, and garlic. Cook over low heat, covered, stirring occasionally, for about 25 minutes or until vegetables are tender.
2. Add beef stock and bring to a boil. Reduce heat, cover, and simmer for about 20 minutes.
3. Pour the soup through a strainer, pressing to extract as much as possible of the vegetable flavors. Discard the solids. Return the soup to the pot.
4. Add rice, sherry, peppers, and salt and freshly ground black pepper. Simmer, partially covered, for about 25 minutes or until rice is tender.
5. Correct seasonings and serve.

Serves 4-6

White Bean and Pepper Soup

The addition of sausage, any kind you like, can make this
chunky soup a hearty one-dish meal.

4 tablespoons butter
2 onions, finely chopped
2 carrots, peeled and chopped
3 garlic cloves, minced
32 fl oz (900 ml or 4 cups) chicken stock
1 tablespoon chopped parsley
1 teaspoon dried thyme
1 bay leaf
12 oz (325 g or 1½ cups) dried white beans, soaked
  overnight
2 green peppers
2 tablespoons olive oil
8 oz (225 g) sausage
salt and pepper to taste

1. Melt butter in a pot and add onions, carrots, and garlic. Cover and cook over low heat for about 20 minutes, until vegetables are tender.
2. Add stock. Stir in the parsley, thyme, and bay leaf. Add the drained beans to the pot. Bring to a boil, then reduce heat and simmer, covered, until beans are tender, about 50 minutes. Discard bay leaf.
3. Remove stems and cores of the peppers. Dice the peppers and sauté in olive oil in a small frying pan, stirring occasionally, until tender but still crunchy, about

15 minutes. With a slotted spoon, transfer the peppers to the soup.

4. Dice the sausage and add to the soup. Cook over medium heat, partially covered, about 15 minutes, or until heated through. Add more water if necessary.

5. Taste for seasonings and serve.

Serves 4-6

Sautéed Green Peppers

This is one of the simplest and best ways to serve green peppers. You can vary it by adding sliced onion or sliced mushrooms to the peppers.

6 medium green peppers, cut into strips
2 tablespoons olive oil
2 cloves garlic, crushed
salt and freshly ground black pepper to taste

1. Heat the oil in a large frying pan. Add the pepper slices, garlic, and salt and pepper. Sauté over medium heat for 5 minutes, stirring occasionally.
2. Cover and cook for another few minutes until pepper strips are tender.

Serves 6-8

Peperonata

This classic Italian pepper and onion sauté makes a wonderful side dish with roast or grilled meat or chicken. It's equally good on its own and just as good hot or cold. It can be kept covered in the refrigerator for a week, but allow it to come to room temperature before serving.

3 green bell peppers
3 red bell peppers
2-3 red or white onions
1-2 cloves garlic, chopped
2 tablespoons olive oil
6 tomatoes, skinned and chopped
salt and pepper

1. Slice the peppers and onions into long strips. Add them to the oil that has been heated in a large frying pan together with the chopped garlic. Sauté over medium heat, stirring frequently, for 10 to 15 minutes, until tender.
2. Mix the tomatoes into the peppers and cook for another 15-20 minutes, until liquid has evaporated. Add salt and freshly ground pepper to taste. Serve hot or at room temperature.

Serves 4-6

Italian Fried Peppers and Vegetables

Fried peppers have a different flavor from grilled or roasted peppers. For this Italian-style vegetable dish, you may vary the proportions of the vegetables and still achieve a delicious result.

4 green or red peppers
3-4 tablespoons olive oil
1 medium-large onion, sliced
4 garlic cloves, finely chopped
1-2 small-medium zucchini (courgettes)
salt and freshly ground black pepper to taste
1 tablespoon chopped fresh basil (½ teaspoon dried)
2-3 teaspoons chopped fresh oregano (½ teaspoon dried)
1½ lbs (750 g) tomatoes, peeled and cut into pieces
3 tablespoons grated Parmesan cheese (optional)

1. Remove stems and seeds from peppers and cut them into 1-inch (2.5 cm) pieces.
2. Heat the oil in a frying pan and sauté the peppers and onion until the onions are soft, about 3-4 minutes. Add garlic and continue to cook for a minute or so.
3. Add zucchini and spices and cook over low heat for another 4-5 minutes until zucchini softens.
4. Add tomatoes and simmer uncovered for about 25 minutes or until tomatoes cook down and take on a thick consistency.
5. Stir in the cheese.

Serves 6-8

Italian Roasted Pepper Casserole

*This can be prepared the day before it is needed and
reheated in a low oven when ready.*

**3 large green (or red) peppers
1 clove garlic, chopped
4 tablespoons pine nuts
1½ oz (40 g or ¼ cup) pitted black olives, cut in pieces
salt and freshly ground black pepper to taste
4-6 tablespoons flavored bread crumbs
2 fl oz (50 ml or ¼ cup) olive oil**

1. Remove seeds and stems from peppers and discard. Cut
   the peppers into strips. Place them in a shallow baking
   dish or casserole. Mix in the garlic, pine nuts, olives,
   salt and pepper.
2. Sprinkle the bread crumbs and the olive oil over the top.
3. Bake uncovered in an oven preheated to 350°F (180°C)
   for 35-40 minutes, stirring occasionally.
4. Serve. Or store in refrigerator if you are planning to use
   it the next day. When ready, reheat the casserole in the
   oven at 300°F (150°C) for about 10 minutes or until
   heated through.

Serves 6

Green Peppers and Rice

A slightly Oriental flavor makes this an especially good side dish.

2 green peppers, chopped
1 tablespoon vegetable or olive oil
3 tablespoons soy sauce
3 tablespoons water
2 tablespoons brown sugar
1 clove garlic, crushed
10 oz (275 g) peas
1½ cups cooked brown rice

1. Heat oil in a large frying pan over medium heat and add peppers. Cook for 10 minutes, stirring frequently.
2. Combine the soy sauce, water, brown sugar, and crushed garlic in a bowl. Add to the frying pan and mix it all together.
3. Reduce heat. Cover and cook for about 5 minutes.
4. Stir in the cooked rice. Heat through and serve.

Serves 4-6

Tunisian Vegetable Stew

*Green pepper is just one ingredient in this lovely stew,
which can be served on couscous or rice to make a quick
and flavorful vegetarian meal.*

2 small-medium onions
2 tablespoons olive oil
half a cabbage, thinly sliced
salt
1 large green bell pepper, cut into thin strips
2 teaspoons ground coriander
½ teaspoon turmeric
¼ teaspoon cinnamon
pinch of cayenne
1 can (28 oz or 800 g) undrained tomatoes, chopped
1 can (16 oz or 450 g) drained chick peas
4 tablespoons currants or raisins (optional)
1 tablespoon fresh lemon juice
salt to taste
grated feta cheese
toasted slivered almonds (optional)

1. Sauté onions in the oil in a large frying pan for 5
   minutes until soft. Add the cabbage, sprinkle with a
   dash of salt, and continue to cook, stirring occasionally,
   for 5 minutes.
2. Add the bell pepper, coriander, turmeric, cinnamon, and
   cayenne and sauté for another minute or two. Stir in the
   tomatoes, chick peas, and currants or raisins. Simmer

183

covered for about 15 minutes or until the vegetables are tender. Add the lemon juice and salt to taste.

3. Sprinkle feta cheese and toasted almonds over the top.

Serves 4

Salad Vegetables

SALAD VEGETABLES

These include lettuce, rocket, chicory, watercress, mustard and cress. There is also celery, which may be eaten raw or sliced in salads. Sharp and savory, celery is an excellent flavoring for soups and stuffings and may also be cooked on its own.

Lettuce, which has been cultivated for thousands of years, comes in hundreds of varieties. Round lettuces are sometimes called head or cabbage lettuce. Butterheads (or Boston) have fragile and loosely packed leaves. Crispheads include iceberg. Looseheads have loose leaves and include many varieties such as lollo rosso and lollo blondo. Cos lettuce includes cos (named for the Greek Island where it was found) and romaine (named by the French who discovered it in Rome). Little Gem is another cos lettuce with a long, erect head. Lamb's lettuce, with spoon-shaped leaves and a nutty flavor, makes a lovely addition to salads.

Rocket or arugula adds a tasty peppery flavor to salads.

Chicory, sometimes called Belgian or French endive, is great eaten raw and even better cooked.

Curly endive and escarole have a robust flavor and texture. The curly endive looks like a frizzy mop, while the escarole is broad-leaved. With their distinctly bitter flavor, they go well with a well-flavored dressing.

Watercress, which grows successfully only in fresh, fast-flowing water, can perk up a salad with its pungent flavor.

Mustard and cress are usually grown together and provide a spicy green in salads or as a garnish.

186

RECIPES for SALAD VEGETABLES

STARTER
Chicory Scoop 188

SOUP
Lettuce Soup 189

SALAD
Rocket and Lettuce Salad 190

SIDE DISHES
Braised Celery 191
Chicory and Carrots 192

Chicory Scoop

*Individual leaves of chicory or Belgian endive make a
natural and deliciously edible means for scooping up a dip
such as salmon mousse or taramosalata. Here is a recipe
for a tapenade dip.*

1. Make a dip.
2. Prepare chicory leaves and arrange them on a platter
   around a bowl containing your chosen dip, such as this
   Provencal selection:

Tapenade Dip:
2 oz (50 g) ripe black olives, pitted
1 oz (25 g) anchovy fillets
1 oz (25 g) tuna fish
1 oz (925 g) capers
1 teaspoon mustard
4-6 tablespoons olive oil
1 tablespoon brandy
freshly ground black pepper to taste

1. Place the pitted ripe olives, anchovy fillets, tuna fish,
   capers, and mustard in a food processer and process
   until you have a smooth paste.
2. Whisk olive oil into the smoothly-blended mixture. Add
   brandy and black pepper.
3. Spoon into a serving bowl.

Serves 8

Lettuce Soup

An abundance of home-grown lettuce can go towards this economical and pleasant soup.

8 oz (225 g) lettuce leaves
1 small onion, finely chopped
1-2 oz (25-50 g) butter
15 fl oz (450 ml or 2 cups) chicken stock
salt and black pepper to taste
sugar and nutmeg to taste
15 fl oz (450 ml or 2 cups) milk
1-2 egg yolks
2 tablespoons cream
croutons to garnish

1. Blanch the washed lettuce leaves in boiling water for 5 minutes. Rinse in cold water and chop the leaves.
2. Melt the butter in a saucepan. Add the chopped onion and fry for 5 minutes. Add the cut-up lettuce, setting aside a few shreds. Pour stock over the mixture and bring to a boil. Season to taste with salt and pepper, sugar and nutmeg.
3. Remove from heat and allow the soup to cool slightly. Process in a liquidizer or food processor. Return to pot. Add milk and reheat at a gentle simmer for 5 minutes.
4. Whisk the egg yolks and cream together. Add a little hot soup and blend thoroughly. Pour the egg mixture into the soup and simmer gently until soup thickens. Do not allow to boil. Add the reserved lettuce shreds just before serving and serve with a bowl of croutons.

Serves 4-6

Rocket and Lettuce Salad

Rocket or arugula, with its pungent flavor, makes a wonderful salad. You can even omit the lettuce and replace it with arugula. Use red peppers for a more colorful salad.

2 large heads of leafy green lettuce such as romaine
2 bunches of arugula
1 lb (450 g) mushrooms, sliced
3 large peppers
Balsamic vinaigrette

1. Wash the inner leaves of the lettuce (discard the outer ones) and dry thoroughly.
2. Remove rocket leaves from their stems, and rinse and dry thoroughly.
3. Remove the stems from the mushrooms reserving them for some other use. Clean mushrooms with damp cloth.
4. Cut the peppers into fine julienne strips.
5. Tear lettuce into bite-size pieces and mix with the rocket in a salad bowl. Add the sliced mushrooms and the peppers. Toss with vinaigrette just before serving.

Serves 6

Braised Celery

Cooking mellows the flavor and texture of this distinctive vegetable, and braising is the best cooking method. This recipe offers a few variations for basic braised celery.

1½ lbs (700 g) celery, trimmed
2 tablespoons butter
salt and freshly ground black pepper
1 tablespoon flour
8 oz (225 ml or 1 cup) chicken stock
Optional: onion, capers, black olives, tomatoes

1. Wash and trim the celery and cut into short lengths. Melt the butter in a large skillet over medium heat.
2. Add the celery and cook, stirring frequently, for about 2 minutes. Season with salt and pepper to taste. Sprinkle in the flour. Cook and stir for another 2 minutes.
3. Mix in the stock. Bring to a boil, then turn heat to low. Cover and cook until celery is tender, about 10-15 minutes. Remove cover. If there is too much liquid, turn up the heat and boil off until you have a thicker texture.
4. To vary this basic recipe, add 2 tablespoons minced onion wtih the celery. After removing cover in step 3, add 1 tablespoon capers, ½ cup chopped black olives, and 1 cup seeded and chopped tomatoes. Cook for 3 minutes and serve.

Serves 4

Chicory and Carrots

Bitter chicory and sweet carrots make an excellent combination and a great accompaniment for chicken or veal.

1 small onion, chopped
1-2 tablespoons butter
1 lb (450 g) chicory
1 lb (450 g) carrots
salt and pepper to taste

1. Saute the onion in butter in a large covered frying pan, over low heat for about 20 minutes.
2. Cut carrots into rings and put them on top of the onions. Simmer, covered, for about another 20 minutes, stirring occasionally.
3. Cut the chicory into rings and add them to the pan. Add seasonings. Simmer until done and serve. Or transfer to a casserole and reheat in oven when ready.

Serves 6

Spinach

SPINACH

Spinach, first cultivated in Persia several thousands of years ago, came to Europe by way of the Arab world. Its popularity grew quickly, perhaps because it is quick and easy to grow as well as easy to cook.

The belief that spinach has a high iron content is untrue, and the Popeye myth needs to be demolished. The iron in spinach occurs in a form that is not as well absorbed by the body as is the iron in meat. However, it is an excellent source of Vitamin A and is also rich in Vitamin C. It is a useful vegetable for salads or for cooking (whether steamed as a vegetable or used as a filling), or in soup.

Among the first cooking greens of spring, spinach is grown also in the winter in many places and is always in good supply. The flat-leafed variety grown by gardeners is tender and requires little or no trimming.

Spinach must be handled with care. Whether you use the round-leaved summer variety or the prickly-leaved winter type, the dark green leaves bruise easily and wilt quickly. After washing several times in cold water to remove sand and grit, place the spinach in a saucepan with no additional water and cook gently, covered, shaking the pan occasionally, for about 10 minutes or less. It is done as soon as it wilts.

RECIPES for SPINACH

SOUPS
Spinach and Yogurt Soup 196
Spinach and Lemon Soup 197
Minted Spinach and Sweet Pea Soup 198
Cream of Spinach Soup 200

APPETIZERS
Spinach-Stuffed Eggs 201
Spinach with Chickpeas 202
Spinach Ramekins 204

SALADS
Spinach Salad 205
Eastern Spinach Salad 206
Tangy Spinach Salad with Pecans 207
Spinach Salad with Pomegranate Seeds 208

ACCOMPANIMENTS
Spinach with Pine Nuts and Raisins 209
Spinach and Tomatoes 210
Spinach with Rice 211
Italian Spinach 212
Viennese Spinach 213
Spinach with Feta Cheese 214
Sesame Spinach 215
Stir-fried Spinach 216
Swiss Spinach Casserole 217

MAIN COURSE
Spinach and Cheese Fritada 218

Spinach and Yogurt Soup

A delightful combination of ingredients produces this splendid spinach soup.

1 lb (500 g) fresh spinach
1 onion, chopped
2 tablespoons olive oil
2 cloves garlic, crushed
40 fl oz (5 cups or 1.1 litres) chicken stock
4 spring onions, finely chopped
4 oz (100 g) rice
salt and pepper to taste
18 fl oz (500 ml) yogurt
2 teaspoons dried mint

1. Wash the spinach and cut into ½-inch (1.5 cm) strips.
2. Place oil in a saucepan and sauté the chopped onion until soft. Add one crushed garlic and cook gently for 2-3 minutes. Add the spinach.
3. Add chicken stock, spring onions, and rice. Season with salt and pepper. Simmer about 20 minutes, until rice is tender.
4. Beat the yogurt together with the other crushed garlic and the mint. Then beat the mixture into the soup and heat through. Be careful not to let the soup boil or it will curdle.

Serves 6

Spinach and Lemon Soup

Turmeric gives this soup an exotic taste of the East.

2 oz (50 g) butter
2 medium onions, chopped
2 lbs (900 g) spinach
rind of 1 lemon
juice of 1 lemon
1 tablespoon turmeric
40 fl oz (1.1 litres) chicken stock
salt and freshly ground black pepper
light cream or yogurt

1. In a large pot, melt the butter and cook the chopped onions in it over low heat until they are soft and translucent, about 10 minutes. Add the washed spinach.
2. Add the lemon rind, lemon juice, turmeric, chicken stock, and the salt and pepper.
3. Bring to the boil, then turn down heat and simmer gently for 30 minutes.
4. Remove from heat, cool, and purée in a food processor or blender.
5. Reheat when ready to serve, and place a spoonful of cream or yogurt in the middle of each plateful of soup.

Serves 6-8

Minted Spinach and Sweet Pea Soup

This rich and delicious mint-flavored soup is a complement to any elegant dinner.

4 tablespoons butter
1 large onion, finely chopped
10 oz (275 g) spinach, chopped
24 fl oz (700 ml or 3 cups) chicken stock
10 oz (275 g) peas (may be frozen)
½ bunch fresh mint (about 2 cups loosely packed leaves)
8 fl oz (225 ml or 1 cup) heavy cream
salt and pepper

1. In a large saucepan, melt the butter and add the onion. Cook over low heat until tender and slightly colored, about 20-25 minutes.
2. Meanwhile, cook the spinach. Drain and squeeze out excess liquid.
3. Pour stock into pan. Stir in the spinach and peas and bring to a boil. Then reduce heat and simmer, partially covered, until peas are tender, about 20 minutes.
4. Rinse mint leaves and pat dry. Add them to the saucepan. Cover and simmer for another 5 minutes.
5. Pour the soup through a strainer reserving the liquid. Transfer the solids to a food processor and add 1 cup of the cooking liquid. Process until smooth.

6. Return the puréed soup to the saucepan. Add the cream and about 1 cup of the additional cooking liquid, until the soup is of the desired consistency.
7. Season with salt and freshly ground black pepper. Simmer to heat through and serve.

Serves 4-6

Cream of Spinach Soup

This makes a comforting winter soup.

1 lb (450 g) spinach
1 oz (25 g) butter
1 small onion, sliced
1 tablespoon cornstarch
30 fl oz (900 ml) milk
2 egg yolks
3 tablespoons cream
salt and pepper to taste
pinch of nutmeg

1. Cook the washed spinach and press it through a sieve.
2. In a saucepan, heat the butter and cook onion slices until tender but not brown.
3. Dissolve the cornstarch in a little of the milk and mix well. Bring to the boil while stirring. Boil for 3 minutes. Strain into the spinach and reheat together with the rest of the milk.
4. Blend the egg yolks and cream together, and mix into it a little of the soup. Then return all to the saucepan. Add salt and pepper and nutmeg.
5. Reheat before serving, being careful not to boil. Spoon a little extra cream into each bowl and serve.

Serves 6-8

Spinach-Stuffed Eggs

*An excellent choice for an hors d'oeuvre or appetizer, this
is very delicious and very attractive.*

8 oz (225 g) spinach, trimmed
8 hard-boiled eggs
1½ oz (35 g) grated Parmesan cheese
2 tablespoons butter
pinch nutmeg
salt and pepper

1. Trim and steam or parboil the spinach. Drain, squeeze
   dry, and chop finely.
2. Peel the cooled eggs and cut them in half lengthways.
   Carefully remove the yolks.
2. Mash the yolks and spinach together. Blend in the
   Parmesan cheese, butter, and nutmeg. Add salt and
   freshly ground pepper to taste. Check seasonings.
3. Spoon the filling into the whites.

Serves 4

Spinach with Chickpeas

Seville is the source for this dish of stewed spinach and chickpeas, although the cumin suggests India. It makes a good hors d'oeuvre or first course—or a side dish.

1 lb (450 g) spinach
6 tablespoons olive oil
4 garlic cloves
2 slices bread (about 2 oz or 50 g), crusts removed
1 heaping teaspoon ground cumin
1 teaspoon sherry vinegar or red wine vinegar
1 tin chickpeas, drained and rinsed
salt and freshly ground black pepper to taste
7 fl oz (200 ml) cold water

1. Wash spinach carefully and discard any tough stalks and damaged leaves. Dry as well as possible and shred.
2. Heat 4 tablespoons of the olive oil in a frying pan and fry both the peeled but whole garlic cloves and the pieces of bread until golden brown. When done, transfer the garlic and bread to a mortar. Add salt and pound to a paste. (Or use a food processor.) Blend in the cumin, vinegar and 2 tablespoons water.
3. Place the remaining 2 tablespoons of oil in a wok or frying pan over high heat. Add the spinach leaves and stir-fry for about 2-3 minutes until spinach begins to soften. Keep stirring the spinach, turning it constantly to give the liquid that oozes out a chance to evaporate.

4. Add the chickpeas, salt and pepper, and water. Bring it to simmer and then stir in the pounded bread and garlic paste. Allow to cook gently for 15 minutes, or until thick and pulpy.
5. Serve right away. Or, better still, allow it to rest overnight and reheat the next day.

Serves 4-6

Spinach Ramekins

*This paté of spinach, sardines and eggs makes a perfect
appetizer. Serve with Italian bread sticks.*

1 lb (450 g) spinach
1 onion, finely chopped
½ teaspoon dried tarragon
2 tablespoons finely chopped parsley
1 hard-boiled egg
4 sardines, boned
2 tablespoons heavy or double cream
salt and pepper
4 anchovy fillets to garnish (optional)

1. Wash the spinach leaves in cold water to remove all the
   grit and soil. Put the wet spinach and the chopped onion
   in a large saucepan with the tarragon and parsley. Cover
   and cook over low heat for 7-10 minutes, until soft.
   Drain thoroughly.
2. Chop the hard-boiled egg and the boned sardines and
   mix with the spinach. Place the mixture in a food
   processor to make a purée. Blend in the cream and
   season to taste with salt and freshly ground black
   pepper.
3. Spoon the mixture into small ramekins or serving dishes.
   Place in refrigerator until chilled and set.
4. To garnish, split the anchovy fillets in half and place
   them on top in a criss-cross pattern.

Serves 4

Spinach Salad

You can vary this salad with avocado. Just omit the tomato and toss with coarsely chopped eggs, onion rings, and a large avocado, diced.

1 lb (450 g) fresh spinach
1 clove garlic
salt
2 tablespoons lemon juice
6 tablespoons olive oil
freshly ground black pepper
2 hard-boiled eggs
1 large tomato
½ red onion or one small one, thinly sliced

1. Wash the spinach thoroughly in cold water. Cut away and discard tough ribs and stems. Drain the spinach leaves, and tear them into bite-sized pieces. Allow to chill in a clean, damp towel.
2. Rub the bottom of a salad bowl with the garlic and sprinkle with salt. Add lemon juice and olive oil and chill the bowl.
3. When ready to serve, add the spinach and sprinkle with pepper. Garnish with hard-boiled eggs cut into wedges, wedges of tomato, and onion rings. Toss lightly and serve.

Serves 6

Eastern Spinach Salad

A refreshing and nutritious salad—with a difference.

10 oz (275 g) fresh spinach, washed and shredded
10 water chestnuts, sliced
3 green onions, sliced
8-10 medium-size mushrooms, sliced
1 cucumber, peeled and thinly sliced
2 tablespoons olive oil
2 tablespoons soy sauce
3 tablespoons lemon juice
1½ tablespoons honey
1 tablespoon sesame seeds, toasted

1. Place the spinach, water chestnuts, green onions, mushrooms, and cucumber slices in a salad bowl.
2. Combine the olive oil, soy sauce, lemon juice, and honey and mix well. Pour over salad and toss.
3. Sprinkle with sesame seeds.

Serves 8

Tangy Spinach Salad with Pecans

An impressive salad and an attractive addition to any meal.

10 oz (275 g) fresh spinach
2½ oz (70 g) pecans, coarsely chopped
12 oz (325 g) cottage cheese
8 oz (225 g or 1 cup) plain yogurt
8-10 tablespoons sugar
3 tablespoons vinegar
1 teaspoon dry mustard
1 tablespoon horseradish
½ teaspoon salt (or less)

1. Wash spinach and drain well. Tear into bite-sized pieces.
2. Place spinach in a salad bowl and combine with pecans and cottage cheese. Mix lightly. Set aside.
3. Combine yogurt, sugar, vinegar, mustard, horseradish and salt to taste. Mix well.
4. Combine the yogurt mixture with the spinach. Toss lightly.

Serves 8

Spinach Salad with Pomegranate Seeds

Red pomegranate seeds accent this unconventional salad from eastern Europe.

1 lb (500 g) spinach
1 tablespoon wine vinegar
2 tablespoons olive oil
1 clove garlic, crushed
¼ teaspoon cayenne pepper
2 spring onions, chopped
a few coriander leaves, chopped
a handful of pomegranate seeds
5 walnut halves, cut into pieces

1. Wash the spinach leaves, removing only the hard stems. Drain and squeeze out the water. Place in a large pan. Cover and steam until leaves crumple. Drain.
2. For the dressing, mix vinegar and oil with the garlic and cayenne pepper, and pour over the spinach.
3. Pull the spinach apart and arrange on a large flat plate. Sprinkle over it the spring onions, coriander, pomegranate seeds, and walnuts.

Serves 4-6

Spinach with Pine Nuts and Raisins

Pine nuts and raisins add an exotic touch to this spinach dish, which can be served hot or cold.

1½ lbs (750 g) spinach
1 onion, chopped
3 tablespoons vegetable oil
3 tablespoons pine nuts
2 tablespoons raisins or sultanas
salt and pepper to taste

1. Wash the spinach, drain, and squeeze out the water.
2. Plump the raisins or sultanas by soaking them in water for 15 minutes.
3. Measure the oil into a large pan and fry the onion until soft. Add the pine nuts and stir until they are lightly browned. Add the raisins or sultanas, drained, and stir it all together.
4. Press the spinach down into the pan. Cover and leave pan on low heat until spinach softens and collapses. Stir in salt and pepper.

Serves 6

Spinach and Tomatoes

Another easy variation on a spinach dish.

10 oz (275 g) fresh spinach
2 cloves garlic, minced
1½ tablespoons olive oil
1 tomato, diced
1 tablespoon raisins

1. Cook spinach in boiling water to cover until tender, about 2 minutes. Drain well and chop coarsely.
2. Sauté garlic in olive oil.
3. Mix in the spinach. Add diced tomato and raisins. Heat through and serve.

Serves 4

Spinach with Rice

A welcome addition to your collection of spinach recipes.

1½ lbs (750 g) spinach
1 large onion, coarsely chopped
4 tablespoons sunflower oil
1 lb (500 g) rice
30 fl oz (900 ml) stock or water
1 teaspoon salt
1 teaspoon sugar
juice of half a lemon
freshly ground black pepper to taste

1. Wash the spinach thoroughly. Drain and cut the leaves coarsely.
2. Using a large pan, fry the onion in the oil until soft. Stir in the rice.
3. Add the stock or water, salt, sugar, and spinach. Mix it all together and cook for about 20 minutes, or until tender.
4. Stir in the lemon juice and pepper before serving.

Serves 6

Italian Spinach

Here is another delightful spinach dish to enhance any dinner.

2 lbs (1 kg) spinach
4 tablespoons olive oil
2 tablespoons butter
1 clove garlic, finely chopped
salt to taste
¼ teaspoon cayenne pepper
Parmesan cheese, coarsely grated

1. Wash and trim the spinach and cut into coarse shreds. Put into boiling water and cook for 30 seconds. Drain well and turn into a baking dish.
2. Heat the olive oil and butter in a frying pan. Add the garlic, salt and cayenne pepper and cook for 5 minutes over low heat.
3. Combine the oil mixture with the spinach. Sprinkle coarsely grated Parmesan cheese over the top and some additional butter, melted. Place under a preheated grill or broiler and brown quickly.

Serves 6

Viennese Spinach

This dish derives its name from the use of sour cream.

2 lbs (1 kg) fresh spinach
1½ tablespoons butter
1 tablespoon flour
4 oz (125 ml or ½ cup) sour cream
1 teaspoon minced onion
salt and pepper

1. Wash the spinach well and cook in a small amount of boiling water, until just tender. Drain thoroughly and chop.
2. Melt the butter in a large pan and stir in the flour. Add the sour cream and onion. Cook and stir until the mixture thickens.
3. Mix in the spinach and heat gently.
4. Season with salt and freshly ground pepper, to taste.

Serves 4

Spinach with Feta Cheese

So simple and so good is this recipe, that you will want to use it frequently.

1 lb (500 g) spinach
2 tablespoons vegetable oil
6 oz (175 g) feta cheese
pepper
pinch of nutmeg

1. Wash the spinach, drain well, and press out excess water.
2. Place oil in a pan and cook the spinach, covered, on low heat for only a few minutes, until the leaves soften.
3. Add the cheese, which has been crushed with a fork. Sprinkle with freshly ground black pepper and nutmeg. Cook and stir for another few minutes, until the cheese melts.

Serves 4

Sesame Spinach

The taste of sesame and the tang of ginger make this an unusual way to prepare spinach. It's a dish that goes particularly well with grilled fish.

1 lb (450 g) fresh spinach
1½ teaspoons sesame seeds
1 tablespoon soy sauce
1 tablespoon dry sherry
1½ teaspoons rice vinegar
½ teaspoon brown sugar
small slice of ginger root
1 tablespoon sesame oil (optional)

1. Wash the spinach well and cut away any tough stems or ribs. Cook in a covered saucepan for about 4 minutes, or until limp. Drain in a colander, pressing to remove excess moisture.
2. Toast the sesame seeds and toss together with the spinach.
3. Make a marinade by combining soy sauce, sherry rice vinegar, brown sugar and ginger root and bringing the ingredients to a boil in a small saucepan. Allow to cool. Remove the ginger and toss the marinade with the spinach.
4. Mix in the sesame oil, if you want to. Serve hot or chilled.

Serves 4

Stir-fried Spinach

Use young and crisp spinach leaves, as fresh from the garden as possible.

1½ lbs spinach
2 cloves garlic, crushed
½ teaspoon salt
3 tablespoons oil
1 tablespoon soy sauce
1 teaspoon sugar (or less)
2 oz (50 g) butter

1. Wash spinach thoroughly in cold water to get rid of sand and grit. Remove rough ribs and discard any bruised leaves.
2. In a large saucepan, heat the oil. Add the garlic and salt and fry over high heat for 30 seconds. Add the spinach and stir constantly for 3 minutes. Stir in the soy sauce, sugar and butter. Continue cooking and stirring for another 2 minutes and serve immediately.

Serves 4

Swiss Spinach Casserole

This is a deliciously flavored casserole which can also be used as a main dish by spooning it over a baked potato and serving together with a salad for a complete meal.

10 oz (275 g) spinach, chopped
1 tablespoon flour
1 small onion, finely chopped
4 fl oz (100 ml or ½ cup) water
6 oz (175 g or ⅔ cup) nonfat dry milk
1 egg white
6 oz (175 g or ⅔ cup) cottage cheese
2 oz (50 g or ½ cup) Swiss cheese, shredded
⅛ teaspoon garlic powder
salt and pepper to taste

1. Cook the spinach and drain well. Chop and place in a large bowl. Sprinkle with flour and mix well.
2. Add remaining ingredients and mix well.
3. Pour into a lightly oiled baking dish or casserole.
4. Bake uncovered for 40 minutes in an oven preheated to 350°F (180°C).
5. Allow to stand for 5 minutes before serving.

Serves 4

Spinach and Cheese Fritada

This is a Mediterranean-style omelet dish that makes a great lunch or supper. It's also useful for buffet meals or picnics. Cottage cheese may be substituted for feta cheese.

14 oz (400 g) spinach
5 eggs
1 medium potato, boiled, peeled, and chopped
7 oz (200 g) feta cheese, mashed
¼ teaspoon nutmeg
pepper to taste
1 tablespoon olive oil

1. Wash the spinach and remove any tough stems or ribs. Drain and place in a covered pan over low heat. Cook just until it wilts and becomes soft. Drain and press out excess water. The leaves may be left whole or coarsely cut.
2. Lightly beat the eggs in a bowl. Add the spinach, potato, cheese, nutmeg and pepper. Stir well.
3. Heat the oil in a frying pan and pour in the spinach and egg mixture. Cook over low heat until the bottom has set, about 10-15 minutes. Then cook under the grill until the omelette is firm and lightly browned.
4. Turn out and serve, either hot or cold, cut into wedges.

Serves 6

Swiss Chard

SWISS CHARD

Swiss chard or chard is often compared with spinach, although the two vegetables are not related. Swiss chard belongs to the beet family and is therefore sometimes called seakale beet or spinach beet. Indeed, it is essentially a beet that is grown for its leaves rather than roots. It is sturdier than spinach and has a stronger and more robust taste than spinach, with an acid-sweet and distinctive flavor. Yet its flavor is more delicate than other greens such as kale or turnip greens. The leaves of the plant are large and dark green, sometimes ruffled, with thick white ribs. Ruby chard has red ribs while those of yellow chard are yellow.

Chard is in season from early June to October. It is easy to grow and deals well with a wide range of temperatures. Because it needs lots of water while growing, it is favored by gardeners in places with high rainfall.

Chard is a good source of calcium and potassium as well as Vitamin C and beta-carotene.

Swiss chard may be cooked on its own, although it is often added to other dishes such as omelets or pies. To cook, wash thoroughly. Cut the stalks across in ½ inch (1.2 cm) slices and add them to the leaves. Cook together in boiling water for about 5 minutes. (Larger pieces of stalks will take longer than the greens to cook.) Serve with butter and salt and pepper. Or chop and sauté with oil and garlic for a minute or two.

RECIPES for SWISS CHARD

ACCOMPANIMENTS

Buttered Swiss Chard

This simple method retains the nutritional value and enhances the flavor.

1 lb (450 g) Swiss chard, with stalks
1½ oz (35g) butter
4 fl oz (100 ml) water or stock
salt and pepper to taste

1. Wash the chard and cut, including the stalks, into 1-inch (2.5 cm) slices.
2. Melt butter in a saucepan. Add the chard, then raise the heat and stir to combine the chard and butter. Add water or stock.
3. Cover the saucepan and cook for about 7 minutes or until tender. If there is too much liquid, remove cover and continue to cook, allowing the water to evaporate.
4. Sprinkle with salt and pepper and serve.

Serves 4

Swiss Chard with Garlic

This extremely easy-to-grow vegetable deserves this extremely easy-to-cook recipe. Beet greens may be substituted for the chard.

10 oz (275 g) fresh Swiss chard
2 tablespoons olive oil
1-2 cloves garlic, minced
salt and pepper to taste

1. Wash well and trim the stems. Shake off excess water. Tear leaves into pieces.
2. Place the oil in a large pan over medium heat and cook the minced garlic for 1-2 minutes. Add the chard and season with salt and pepper.
3. Cook, stirring until the leaves wilt, about 3-5 minutes.

Serves 3

Swiss Chard with Pine Nuts

This is a sweet dish, which can also be made with spinach.
It goes well with savory meats.

2 lbs (1 kg) Swiss chard
2 tablespoons olive oil
1-2 cloves garlic, minced
8 tablespoons (½ cup) pine nuts
8 tablespoons (½ cup) currants (or raisins)
salt and pepper to taste

1. Wash chard thoroughly. Bring water to a boil in a large pot. Chop stems and cook until they are almost tender, about 5 minutes. Add the chopped leaves and continue to cook together for another few minutes until both are tender. Drain and squeeze dry.
2. Place oil in a large frying pan over medium-low heat and cook the garlic until it begins to color, about 5 minutes.
3. Add pine nuts and cook and stir for another minute. Add the chard, currants (which have been soaked in warm water for 10 minutes) and salt and pepper.
4. Continue cooking and stirring for about 2 minutes. Serve hot or at room temperature.

Serves 4-6

Pasta with Swiss Chard Sauce

Served with garlic bread and a salad, this pasta dish, with its excellent green sauce, makes a complete meal.

1 lb (450 g) Swiss chard, tough stalks removed
1 bunch watercress
2 garlic cloves, grated
1 tablespoon olive oil
salt and freshly ground black pepper to taste
¼ teaspoon nutmeg
5 oz (150 g or ¾ cup) ricotta cheese
1 lb (450 g) pasta (penne, fusilli, macaroni, or shells)
grated Parmesan cheese or pine nuts (optional)

1. Wash the Swiss chard and watercress well and chop coarsely.
2. Place oil in a saucepan and sauté the garlic until golden, about 1 minute. Add the chard and watercress. Sauté, stirring frequently, until the greens are wilted but still bright green. Sprinkle with salt, pepper, and nutmeg. Remove from heat.
3. Purée the mixture in a blender or food processor together with the ricotta cheese, until smooth.
4. Add the pasta to a large pot of boiling water and cook uncovered until done (*al dente*). Drain. Toss the pasta with the sauce in a warmed serving bowl.
5. Top with Parmesan or toasted pine nuts and serve.

Serves 4-6

Chard Stalks with Parmesan

Here is a good way to prepare the thick midribs of Swiss chard, whether thick- or thin-stemmed, while reserving the tender leaves for another recipe.

1½ lbs (700 g) chard stems
2-4 tablespoons butter
salt and freshly ground black pepper
about 1 cup freshly grated Parmesan cheese

1. Cut the leaves away from the stems and keep them for another recipe. Simmer or steam the chard stems until tender, about 5-10 minutes. Drain and rinse with cold water to stop the cooking. Then drain again and dry.
2. Place the stems in a buttered oven casserole or baking dish. Dot with butter and sprinkle with salt and pepper. Distribute about two-thirds of the cheese over the stems.
3. Place casserole in an oven preheated to 450°F (230°C) and bake until cheese just begins to turn brown, about 10 to 15 minutes. Sprinkle with the remaining cheese and serve.

Serves 4

TABLE OF EQUIVALENT WEIGHTS AND MEASURES

Teaspoon and Tablespoon Measurements are level.

LIQUID EQUIVALENTS
1 litre = 1000 ml = 1¾ Imperial pints = 2 US pints = 4 cups
          600 ml = 1 Imperial pint = 1¼ US pint = 2½ cups
½ litre = 500 ml = ¾ Imperial pint = 1 US pint = 2 cups
          300 ml = ½ Imperial pint = 1¼ cups
¼ litre = 250 ml = 8 fl oz = ½ US pint = 1 cup
          150 ml = 5 fl oz = ⅔ cup
          100-125 ml = 3½-4 fl oz = ⅓-½ cup

WEIGHTS
28 g = 1 oz
110 g = 4 oz or ½ cup
225 g = 8 oz or 1 cup
450 g = 16 oz or 1 lb
1 kg = 2 lbs

SOME INGREDIENT MEASUREMENTS
fresh breadcrumbs   3½ oz (100 g) = 2 cups
grated Parmesan cheese 1¾ oz (48 g) = ¼ cup
butter   8 oz (250 g) = 1 cup
cheese, grated   2 oz (50-60 g) = ½ cup
flour   1 lb (500 g) = 3¾ cups
                         5 oz (150 g) = 1 cup
rice   8 oz (250 g) = 1 cup
sugar   2 oz (50-60 g) = ⅓ cup
vegetables, chopped, raw 4 oz (125 g) = 1 cup